PTSD Recovery Workbook for Teens

PTSD Recovery Workbook for Teens

Strategies to Reduce Stress, Build Resiliency, and Overcome Trauma

Dr. Stephanie Bloodworth, PsyD

ROCKRIDGE
PRESS

First Rockridge Press trade paperback edition 2022

Rockridge Press and the Rockridge Press logo are trademarks or registered trademarks of Callisto Media Inc. and/or its affiliates in the United States and other countries and may not be used without written permission.

For general information on our other products and services, please contact our Customer Care Department within the United States at (866) 744-2665, or outside the United States at (510) 253-0500.

Manufactured in the United States of America

Interior and Cover Designer: Linda Kocur
Art Producer: Maya Melenchuk
Editor: Alexis Sattler
Production Editor: Caroline Flanagan
Production Manager: Riley Hoffman

All illustrations used under license from Shutterstock

Author photo © Anchor & Oar Photography June 2020

Paperback ISBN: 978-1-63878-302-2 | eBook ISBN: 978-1-63878-248-3

10 9 8 7 6 5 4 3 2 1 0

This workbook belongs to:

_____

Contents

Introduction

Hello, and welcome to this workbook. These pages are meant to provide you with a space to learn about and work through post-traumatic stress disorder. You may have a formal diagnosis, or perhaps you strongly suspect it following a traumatic experience. You can use this workbook along with treatment and discuss your work here with your therapist. If having a therapist is not an option for you right now, you can still use this workbook as a source of support. The tools and activities in this book are designed to help you establish a sense of safety and stability, process and express your experiences, and figure out your personal values to guide your growth going forward.

We're going to talk a lot about you, the things that have challenged you, and who you want to be. So, it's only fair that I share about myself and my experience. My name is Stephanie Bloodworth. I grew up in a dysfunctional home where I was constantly put down for things I couldn't control. My response to that mistreatment was a curiosity to learn as much as I could. I wanted to understand, well, *everything*! I wanted to understand why people did and said the things they did. I wanted to know how to navigate and move forward from any situation. It took many years of study and work, but I now get to help other people understand complicated situations and figure out what they want to do next. I have a doctoral degree in clinical psychology, and I work as a marriage and family therapist in Houston, Texas.

I began working with teenagers during my master's degree training when I worked at a shelter for at-risk and unhoused youth. It was an absolute honor to work with teens facing mental health issues, substance issues, interpersonal challenges, and figuring out who they wanted to be in the world, on top of housing insecurity.

I've continued to work with teens throughout my career. I help them sort through what they've been through as they look forward to who they are becoming. What helps me the most in my work with teens like you is that I haven't forgotten what it was like to be one. I value what you have to say. As teens, you may not have the same experience and learned wisdom as adults, but you have valid and valuable insights. Your feelings and experiences are important.

I have a deep respect for what teens face. The world can feel chaotic. It's hard to watch friends and people all over the world suffer. Sometimes you're the one who suffers. Violence, abuse, struggle, people being treated like they're less than human—it can hurt to even think about. You lose connections you thought were forever. You feel pushed to just "move on" and "think on the bright side," but the more you ignore your grief, pain, and confusion, the worse it seems to get. In the meantime, you may be told by adults that what you went through "wasn't a big deal" and that it "won't matter when you're older." Even if it's true that this will matter less when you're older, it matters now. And that's what counts.

So, let's do something different here. Let's make a space where you can feel safe to be honest about what you went through and how you're doing. Where you're safe to say it's the end of the world when it feels like the end of the world you thought you had. Where I can help you mourn and then encourage you to think about the world that can come next. You are far from alone: Many people, including teens, are dealing with similar issues and working toward something better.

I want to give you the information and support you need to rebuild safety and peace, heal, and create an even better life for yourself. I want to help you learn how to manage your symptoms and feelings by giving you new tools and the space to write and reflect on your experience. Ultimately, I want to help you learn more about who you are and who *you* want to be so you can start growing into that person. No matter what you went through, that's *not* the end of your story. Let's work on building what comes next.

A Note for Readers

You've been through a lot in life, even without your traumatic experience. The teen years are a tough mix of learning about yourself, others, and the world around you while also dealing with the pressures of school or work or whatever else you have on your plate. You're experiencing lots of emotions and events for the first time while also looking forward to building your future. And now? Now you're still expected to do all those things while dealing with the fact that your views of yourself, others, and the world around you have changed.

Your traumatic experience may have left you with many difficult and lasting effects, some of which you might not even realize are related to PTSD. You might not be sure what to think or feel. You might be experiencing an out-of-control swirl of unwanted thoughts and feelings. With PTSD, it can be hard to feel like life can ever be good again. This struggle doesn't have to be forever. You can feel good again; in fact, you can feel stronger and better than ever before.

Whatever you've been through, and whatever it is you're struggling with, this is a safe and judgment-free zone. My goal with this book is to help you feel supported and empowered. You'll work on establishing safety and stability for yourself in your present environment as much as possible. You'll learn ways to work with your thoughts and feelings without becoming overwhelmed or controlled by them. You'll practice telling your story in a way that gets you unstuck from your trauma. You'll learn how to express yourself and advocate for yourself, even around people who don't respect your boundaries. And finally, you'll explore what's important to you and your goals for the future.

The world can be unpredictable, but this workbook was created to help you gain the healing and adaptability you'll need to handle any surprises and obstacles that life throws your way. This ability might feel far from where you are right now, but with regular attention and deliberate work on healing, I feel confident you can get there.

You've been through something serious, and it's important to take your healing just as seriously. You deserve your own consideration on a regular basis. Making time to handle your PTSD as a normal part of your daily schedule will make healing part of your daily experience. Maybe you'd like to read one section a week and then practice the activities that follow every day throughout the rest of the week. Maybe it'll work better for you to set a timer for, say, fifteen minutes a day and read and do what you can until the timer goes off. Whatever pace works for you is great. Just check in with yourself throughout the process and see if what you are doing is working. You may need to adjust your schedule to fit your needs.

Although just reading about PTSD isn't likely to suddenly make all your symptoms go away, you will gradually heal as you learn and practice these new skills and tools. The important thing is to try and prioritize your needs regularly. This workbook can become part of a healthy self-care ritual, where you add on to good habits or develop new ones to be kind to yourself. Maybe you can set aside some time at the end of your day or over the weekend just to take care of yourself. During this time, you might choose to tune in to your senses, engage in some healthy movement, and spend some time caring for your mental health. You can follow up by treating yourself—maybe by watching a fun show or listening to your favorite songs. Despite how difficult and challenging your experience was, healing can be something you look forward to. You've got so many amazing and wonderful possibilities ahead of you. If that's a hard hope for you to carry right now, I'm happy to hold it for you until you're ready.

A Note for Guardians

Hello to the people raising and taking care of teens! Whether you are a parent, sibling, extended family member, guardian, or otherwise trusted adult, your role is valuable. A healthy connection to caregivers is an important factor in every teen's healing and growth. Allow this section to serve as a starting point for some gentle conversations with the teen owner of this book. Please share this section with them or read it together so everyone can think about the best way to move forward. Here are some decisions for you to discuss and decide together:

- What kind of privacy can your teen expect surrounding their work in this workbook? Although you may want to know the details of how they are doing and if they are having any problems, it's important they grow in their sense of personal capability and what they want to share. You may be a perfectly safe, nonjudgmental, non-shaming person, but giving them space to practice assertive communication for others who may overstep their boundaries is so valuable. They may also need more time to process before they are ready to express themselves to you. My advice would be to work together to figure out how you can help them and know if there are any problems while also giving them a sense of personal privacy.

- Will they check in with you to review their progress? They might want to talk to you about what activities they're working on and what they have learned. This lets you know how they are doing and what they're struggling with; additionally, their ability to share what they have learned with someone they trust helps them learn and process even better. This is a great way for your teen to feel supported and encouraged in the work they are doing. Talk about when and how they will check in with you or share their progress.

- Will they go through this book with the guidance of a mental health clinician? If your teen is working with a therapist, it may be helpful to follow their guidance as part of treatment. If they don't have a therapist at this time, what might be the best time and pacing for them to work through this book? As a caregiver, your input and support in making this book part of their regular healing and self-care will help. How might you help them spend time consistently on their healing? Together, discuss what kind of schedule will help them best learn and practice the tools in this workbook.

- How will they let you know if they need help or are feeling overwhelmed? If they have difficulty communicating in those moments, what signs should you look for, and how can you best respond? Discussing these concerns together will help you keep your teen safe and cared for throughout their healing process. By preparing for the possibility that your teen will feel overwhelmed, you'll be more ready when the need arises.

As you prepare to support the owner of this workbook, please also consider your own needs as a caregiver. You may be feeling your own mix of emotions and difficulty because of what your teen has experienced. You may have experienced the trauma as well. You might feel sadness, anger, and grief as your teen learns to express how their trauma has affected them. As they begin to feel more comfortable sharing with you, you might learn things you didn't know before. The best way to be resourceful and supportive for them in those moments is to be present, acknowledge their experiences, and support them in what they need.

To be most effective requires you to take care of yourself, too. Are you prioritizing basic needs like sleep, eating, hydrating, and engaging in activities that bring you joy? Do you have people you can trust to support you—maybe even a mental health clinician of your own? Are you being kind to yourself, even when you struggle? Teens learn strongly from the example we set as trusted adults. This doesn't mean you have to be "perfect." Instead, allow yourself to be human. Allow yourself to have a hard time sometimes. And, please, allow yourself to care for yourself and get any support you may need.

How to Use This Book

As you begin reading, you'll notice different themes and types of content throughout this book. The information and activities are organized to build on each other, so each chapter provides a solid foundation for the chapters to come. Even so, take the opportunity to read and work on the activities in the ways that work best for you. Here's a basic rundown:

- **CHAPTER 1** will explore the history of PTSD as well as different forms of traumatic experiences. You'll learn more about the symptoms of PTSD and how they can impact your teen years. You'll also prepare for your healing journey by considering obstacles you might encounter.

- **CHAPTER 2** is intended to help you understand and work through your trauma. You'll learn why you are experiencing the symptoms you have and how you can manage them.

- **CHAPTER 3**'s focus is to help you heal, process, and move on from your traumatic experience. You'll work on establishing as much safety and security as you can and build valuable coping skills.

- **CHAPTER 4** will look at your relationships with yourself and others. You'll learn how to identify your needs, establish boundaries, and protect yourself from unhealthy relationships.

- **CHAPTER 5** will help you look forward to your future and feel more prepared, even when life isn't predictable. You'll learn more about adaptability, acceptance, and the way your healing can impact you and even others for the better.

Each topic is followed by one or two activities related to the information you just learned. This way, you have an opportunity to put that information into practice. These exercises can be done as many times as you'd like—this will help you grow in your ability to manage your PTSD. You don't have to follow these activities exactly as written. In fact, if they inspire you to create your own ways of understanding and practicing the material, that's great. The goal is to find manageable tools for processing and moving forward from your traumatic experience.

In this book, you'll find sections called "Midway Check-In" and "Closing Check-In." These will encourage you to check in with yourself, think more about what you've learned, congratulate yourself on the work you've done, and listen to your needs. After all, working on PTSD can be tiring or upsetting at times. I've also included stories about teens who have experienced something traumatic in different areas. These stories are modified, and the names are changed for privacy, but they come from the experiences of real teens who have given me permission to share them with you. There is no singular way to work through trauma, so don't feel discouraged if your healing process is different. It's our hope that, by hearing how someone else has dealt with something similar and worked through it, you may feel encouraged, too.

CHAPTER 1

The Truth about PTSD

Let's get started! You're going to find a lot of information here as we discuss the background of PTSD, how it forms, what it can look like, and the specific ways it can impact teenagers. We will talk about how PTSD impacts your nervous system and your whole body and why that can make moving forward hard after a traumatic experience. And you'll get the chance to evaluate how you've been feeling and decide whether seeking support from a therapist is a good next step.

This chapter is the longest in the book, so take your time and feel free to skip around if that works best for you. Knowing more about PTSD can help you understand what is going on for you and remind you that you aren't alone in this. The most important thing is that you feel safe as you read through this information. We'll be exploring different kinds of trauma that can result in PTSD. There are no explicit descriptions of traumatic events, but please go through this section slowly and pay attention to the signs your body sends you as you read. If you notice you are beginning to feel upset or uncomfortable, or your body is feeling numb or "buzzy," for example, these could be signs that the information is triggering your own trauma experience and responses. Feel free to slow down, skip around, or stop reading whenever you feel like it. You can also use the physical grounding exercise (see page 21) and check-in (see page 22) at the end of this chapter at any time. This book is here for you to use in ways that support you.

Here's a list of the topics we'll talk about in this chapter. If you want to put some of them off for another time when you feel more prepared, that's okay. The information will be here whenever you are ready. You can check off the topics below as you read them if you want to keep track. You can also put a star next to ones you found particularly helpful or ones you'd like to revisit later. This is your book: Make notes anywhere you want, underline what you want, or highlight whatever is interesting to you.

☐ What Is PTSD?

☐ PTSD: Fact vs. Fiction

☐ Types of Trauma That Can Cause PTSD

   ☐ Political Instability or Social Upheaval

   ☐ Childhood Abuse/Neglect

   ☐ Sexual Abuse or Assault

☐ Physical Assault or Violence

☐ Severe Accidents or Health Crises

☐ The Impacts of PTSD on Teens

☐ PTSD Self-Evaluation

☐ Identifying Your Healing Barriers

What Is PTSD?

PTSD, or post-traumatic stress disorder, is a mental health condition that forms when the effects of a traumatic event continue to affect someone long after the event has ended. PTSD is usually the result of an alarming situation, where the brain experienced a spike in stress hormones and is now having trouble moving out of protection mode. Once someone's brain gets stuck in this protection mode, it signals to the rest of the body that the danger continues. Because of this, PTSD doesn't just affect someone's thinking and emotions; it can also cause physical symptoms such as increased heart rate, shallow breathing, and muscle tension. As a result of this feeling of danger, the person may avoid processing or thinking about the event to work through it.

It's totally normal to feel upset and rattled by a tragic, upsetting, or extremely scary experience for some time after it's over. Our brains need time and space to understand what happened and figure out what to do next. Over time, though, we usually find a way to move forward in healthy ways. When that healthy and adaptive movement forward never happens, PTSD forms.

People with PTSD may find themselves feeling like what happened is still happening, or just happened, even months or years later. They might have sudden, uncontrollable memory flashbacks, where it feels like the past is happening in the present, or the emotional form of flashbacks, where they feel exactly how they did during the event. Flashbacks may include the clear memory of the event or just the feelings from the event. People with PTSD might feel anxious and on edge all the time, worried about all kinds of dangers even if those dangers aren't present. They can feel numb and have depressive symptoms, as if they and the world around them don't have a purpose, or they may feel separated from a world they no longer relate to. Nightmares and trouble eating and sleeping can also happen with PTSD. Because of how alarming and upsetting their experience was, people with PTSD may try to avoid anything that could remind them of their trauma, even if it's something that's usually pleasant, like spending time with friends or visiting a park.

There is also a form of PTSD that can develop not because of a single alarming event but from smaller events stacking up over time. This might start with a very difficult and traumatic environment someone must live in for a very long time or a series of events that challenge someone's ability to think about themselves and the world around them in a healthy way. Over time, that person can have trouble knowing what to think about themselves, how to get along with others without hurting themselves, how to manage their emotions, and how to cope with challenging experiences. This is called complex post-traumatic stress disorder, or C-PTSD.

A Brief History of PTSD

The experience of being stuck in the effects of a traumatic event has been documented since the beginning of history. Reports from ancient Assyrian armies included signs of PTSD among their soldiers between 1300 and 609 BCE. Many centuries later came the first U.S. recognition of PTSD symptoms, identified by researchers and clinicians treating Vietnamese civilians who had witnessed and experienced the traumatic effects of the Vietnam War firsthand. Soon after that, doctors in the United States noticed the lingering effects of war trauma on Vietnam War veterans, leading to the term "post-traumatic stress disorder." As a result, PSTD is still sometimes inaccurately considered a condition specific to combat veterans. Despite the origin of our understanding of PTSD relating to Vietnamese civilians, a 2021 study led by Yvette Young reported that comparatively little research and treatment to date focuses on Vietnamese civilians and their treatment needs.

Since then, the world has also recognized that events beyond combat exposure can contribute to PTSD. There are countless traumatic events and disasters other than war that can leave lasting negative effects on those who experience them.

As researchers continue to learn more, they've also begun exploring complex post-traumatic stress disorder, or C-PTSD, which may form when someone is exposed to a long-term traumatic environment or, alternatively, several traumatic events, the effects of which stack over time. Researchers and clinicians continue to study and treat people who show signs of this complex form of PTSD, paving the way to a better understanding and ability to help people who have experienced various forms of trauma.

PTSD Fact vs. Fiction

There are many misconceptions about what PTSD is and what it means for those who have it. Here are the facts to address the myths:

"PTSD is something only veterans get." Anyone who experiences a disturbing event might develop the disorder if they do not have access to the resources and opportunities to appropriately process and heal from their experience.

"PTSD only happens when someone is killed, or something explodes." Getting stuck in a traumatic experience can happen no matter the scale of the event. Not all traumatic experiences may seem obvious, but they can still leave a lingering impact. Drawn-out psychological abuse in a close relationship, for example, can be traumatic and cause a form of PTSD.

"PTSD is guaranteed for some events." Not everything that is potentially traumatic will traumatize you. Sometimes you go through something awful and find you're able to move forward. PTSD usually forms when someone doesn't have the right resources and support to work through the experience effectively.

"If you're upset after something happens, it's PTSD." PTSD is different from grief. It's normal to have a hard time after when something negative throws you off. But if it's been a while and that pain or memory hasn't changed in a healing way, those might be signs of PTSD. Clinicians consider the time frame when making a diagnosis.

"If you have PTSD, that's just your life now." PTSD does not have to be lifelong, and it gets better when treated appropriately. Unfortunately, many people with PTSD go without the help needed for their healing.

"Healing will make things go back to how they used to be." Treatment doesn't cut trauma out like it never happened. Healing means figuring out how to understand what happened, paying respect to how it affected you, and finding healthy ways to move forward. There is no such thing as going back to how things were before, but you can create a new normal. The new normal can even be better, more meaningful, and more fulfilling than the old normal.

"PTSD and healing are predictable." PTSD and healing look different from person to person. Everyone will have their own experiences and heal on their own time line.

[Marta's Story]

Marta's city was hit by an earthquake and its aftershocks. She and her immediate family were okay, but Marta's grand-parents, aunts, uncles, and cousins had to leave their homes because of the damage. They came to stay with Marta's family to recover and figure out what to do next. Marta was glad her family could help, but people were everywhere in her house all the time. She lost her private space to think or do her schoolwork. Marta felt like she couldn't talk about how scared or upset she was about the earthquake because the people around her seemed to have it worse.

Months after everyone could go back home, Marta still felt scared, upset, and unsafe in her house. She had night-mares about the ground shaking, wondering if her family would live through the catastrophe, but she didn't feel like she could talk to anyone about her experiences. Marta went back to school and hoped being busy would help, but her usual motivation for school was gone. When the memories returned, she'd lose focus. Sometimes her heart would start racing out of nowhere. Marta began to feel like nothing was real in the world around her, except for the moments of panic. She finally broke down to her parents about every-thing. They brought her to a therapist, and Marta was able to talk about her experience, learn about PTSD, and start feeling unstuck.

Types of Trauma That Can Cause PTSD

The field of mental health has come a long way since PTSD was considered only a combat veteran's experience. Anyone can experience and become stuck in trauma, regardless of age or occupation. This can include general events, like natural disasters, or targeted events, like assault and abuse. Not everything that can be traumatic will necessarily traumatize someone—it depends on each person's experience. What tends to be consistent about trauma is that people feel like there is a distinct *before* it happened and *after* it happened and that their view of themselves or the world has now changed. People who have lived in traumatic events since childhood may not get a sense of before and after, but their views of themselves, others, and the world are nonetheless altered.

This section will explore several different types of potentially traumatic experiences. Some types of trauma may sound more severe than others, but it's important to remember that all experiences are valid and unique to the individual. What matters is not the amount or cause of trauma, but that everyone deserves the opportunity to process and heal. Whether your trauma looks like one of the circumstances described in this workbook or is very different, anything you struggle with deserves support.

Political Instability or Social Upheaval

Governments and social norms dictate everything from what you learn in school to the condition of roads you take to get there, and from how you express yourself to how you think about others. Political battles can pit communities against each other and bring combat and destruction to a neighborhood. You might have lived under constant occupation and had your daily options limited to what was allowed. You might have faced persecution and threats to your survival simply because of who you are or what you believe. Living in constant threat of danger can set the tone for what you expect from others in the world. As a result, you might have trouble trusting others and feeling comfortable developing who you are. You may struggle with violence you've experienced and witnessed while being disconnected from supports that could help you heal. A large part of trauma is feeling isolated, and political instability and social upheaval can cause both isolation and a threat to survival.

To escape oppression and instability, people may emigrate to new countries for safety and better opportunities. Whether as a refugee or a different immigrant category, moving to a new culture can be overwhelmingly difficult and contribute to the trauma. This process may involve leaving behind family, friends, and a community you understood. You may have difficulty getting used to living life in a very different environment. Figuring out how to think of your cultural identity can be an additional challenge. People in the new country may be hostile to refugees and immigrants. These challenges to stability can prolong the negative effects of your traumatic experience.

Childhood Abuse/Neglect

You learned an astonishing amount of information in childhood without realizing it. Based on what your caregivers modeled and told you, you learned about your worth, how to interact with others, and how to understand the world. If your childhood included abuse and/or neglect, you could suffer as a kid and take away inappropriate lessons that leave you vulnerable to unhealthy future situations. Physical abuse hurts and can create a deep fear of the world and other people. Psychological and emotional abuse damages your view of yourself and others, including teaching you that your value and worth are based on certain conditions when it absolutely is not. Whether purposeful or unintentional, neglect can teach you to ignore and devalue your physical, medical, and emotional needs.

The world is challenging and can be difficult, but childhood is a time we should be experiencing the positive connections and encouragement that will help us overcome challenges. If you were taught to feel ashamed about who you are, for example, you might not make decisions that honor and respect yourself, and instead, put yourself in danger. Not knowing how to value yourself can make it difficult to avoid traumatic experiences going forward. No parents or caregivers are perfect, and all will make mistakes occasionally, but there is a big difference between a mistake and the abuse or neglect of a child. Caregivers and parents are charged with raising a whole new human and building them up to be their best, not breaking them down.

Sexual Abuse or Assault

Sexuality is one of many aspects of our lives that can offer us connection, expression of our feelings and desires, and intimate insight into who we are. How you engage with yourself and others sexually should be an empowered and respectful decision. Being forced, manipulated, or pressured into sexual activity is wrong, and it negatively impacts your sense of self and connections with others. Sexual abuse can come with or without threats or physical force. Anyone who uses their power or authority to violate someone's boundaries or force another person to engage sexually is acting in an abusive way. Additionally, people might agree to unwanted sexual activity because they feel like they can't say no, either because they are intimidated by others or because they have never been supported in setting boundaries that might allow them to say no.

Traumatic sexual experience goes beyond what you label it. Whether you classify experiences as rape or sexual assault typically matters for only one context: in the court of law. But trauma doesn't care about what the legal world calls what you went through—it affects you regardless. You are allowed to decide that a sexual experience affected you negatively, was unwanted, or was not good. Whatever the circumstances, an upsetting sexual experience is worth getting support for.

Physical Assault or Violence

Physical bodies are amazing. They move with purpose and specificity. They rebuild and recover so we can function. They constantly take in and process a great deal of information about the outside world. And from the inside, they help us form a sense of who we are and who we want to be.

When someone harms your body, you register pain messages both physically and psychologically as your mind tries to figure out what is happening and why. You may have injuries from an assault that continue to interfere with your daily life. You can also be impacted strongly by seeing someone else experience assault and violence, especially if you identify with them in some way. Sometimes you may wonder if you will survive an active assault, and part of your brain kicks in to try to increase your chances of living. This is the body's "fight, flight, or freeze" survival response. If you survive but continue to feel unsafe, it can be hard to engage with the world around you because your brain may still be in this survival mode.

Violence does not need to threaten your life to be traumatic. Physical pain and discomfort are pain and discomfort, regardless. Additionally, the people hurting you may be people you know and care about deeply. Understanding how the violence fits into what you believe about your relationship with these people can be difficult. If you can't avoid them; the violence can warp your view of what healthy engagement with others looks like.

Severe Injuries or Health Crises

Humans tend to be creatures of habit, and they like a general sense of stability. People like to expect things will go as planned. You usually don't expect to experience a traumatic injury or a health crisis that either threatens your survival or changes the way you live your life going forward. So, if you experience or witness a severe injury or a car crash, it's natural to feel shocked and shaken. If you or someone you care about has a health crisis, you might feel stuck worrying about survival and how your life will have to change.

Witnessing or experiencing severe injuries may challenge how safe you feel continuing to live your life after the event. Your worries may begin as reasonable reactions, but they may grow too large and take over your ability to function, even though you are, in fact, safe again. If you experience an injury or have a different health crisis, you might have to change your everyday activities. You might be used to feeling very independent and now need help from others to do simple things. Your grief and desire for the way things used to be can override your ability to move forward and leave you feeling stuck.

The Impacts of PTSD on Teens

The teenage years are an extremely important and formative part of life. Famed neuroscientist Dr. Dan Siegel studied and reported that the adolescent brain is flooded with many amazing chemicals as it grows and you learn more about yourself and the world. Part of what makes being a teenager so complicated can be that you're experiencing so many things for the first time without knowing how to handle it all.

"Your time as a teenager is important and worth respecting."

The prefrontal cortex, which is the part of your brain that's good at making long-term decisions, will continue developing until you're about twenty-five.

That brain development will take into account a lot of what you are going through now. Because of this, spending your adolescent years with PTSD can negatively affect you both now, while this storm of new experiences is happening, and if not taken care of, into the future. The sooner you can handle your difficult situation, the sooner you can focus again on the things you enjoy and the goals you hope to accomplish. Conversely, the longer you struggle with your experiences, the more difficult it will be to move forward, both now and as an adult.

Your time as a teenager is important and worth respecting. PTSD isn't something that just haunts your thoughts while leaving the rest of your life unaffected—it affects everything if untreated. This section will explore the emotional, mental, and physical impacts of PTSD, especially for teens.

Emotional

Your emotions help you understand what's working for you and what's not. Processing your feelings by figuring out what you feel and why gives you the information to make changes. For people with PTSD, processing their emotions can be difficult because the main system online is dealing with survival. In this mode, emotions like fear and anger get top consideration. Fear and anger help you respond quickly to dangerous situations, but they can also cover deeper feelings, such as pain, grief, and sadness. When you're faced with a lot of negative emotions, you may try to stuff them down because they are so uncomfortable. The problem with that is you can't pick which feelings you do or don't want to have. Either you are open to the full range of human experience, pleasant or unpleasant, or you're likely to feel numb or spill over when unpleasant and painful things become too much to hold.

Your teenage years are already emotionally complex; after all, you're processing many new experiences. As you learn more about the world and yourself, you have the chance to manage your emotions so they aren't constantly controlling you

PTSD complicates this normal process by increasing your pain and negativity. This can be an extremely overloading and overwhelming experience. If you try and stuff it down, it ends up controlling you by holding you back from your everyday life and opportunities for growth and joy. You might find yourself lashing out when the pain forces its way out, only to regret it later. Emotional regulation is hard enough *without* PTSD. With PTSD, some people feel they won't ever stop crying if they start to talk about upsetting things. Or that if they express their anger, they will destroy everything. When processed appropriately, though, feelings can tell you what is going on inside and allow you to move forward. Treatment focused on emotional regulation often helps people learn how to feel calm and secure so they can slowly work through all the feelings that have been swirling for so long.

Mental

The "mind" is a strange and fascinating structure. We can scientifically understand the links between brain cells and how they process information, but there is still something that science has not yet come to understand: consciousness. We understand the brain, but the mind is something extraordinary. Dr. Dan Siegel and experts from many fields met at a summit to discuss this, and even they struggled to agree on how to define the "mind." In the end, their basic idea was this: Your mind is the structure from which you understand yourself and the world around you. Your mind stores and makes meaning from all your experiences, drawing conclusions about everything from what the color purple looks like to what purpose you've found in your life.

Your brain has been growing rapidly your whole life, but your teen years see a steep growth in how you see your sense of self and the world around you. Your brain will continue to form its prefrontal cortex, the part needed to think responsibly about decisions, as well as think abstractly about philosophy and its application to humanity, into your twenties. Your experiences as a teen really matter for this brain growth.

When you have PTSD, your brain has made connections necessary for survival. This can look like hypervigilance: always being on edge because you feel like something bad could happen at any moment. You might experience paranoia and mistrust people and situations that would normally feel fine because your thoughts communicate that anyone and anything *could* be dangerous. These thoughts are fueled strongly by your brain's limbic system, which is responsible for many of your emotional experiences, as well as your basal ganglia, which is a part of the brain responsible for those fight, flight, or freeze reflexes. And when these parts are fired up? The prefrontal cortex takes a back seat, so your ability to plan ahead and think wisely is limited—PTSD has your thoughts focused on survival in the moment. PTSD puts you out of control of your own mental space.

Physical

PTSD is a mental health condition, but it also affects physical well-being. The prime suspect? Cortisol. Cortisol is the hormone released in your body that helps you navigate stressful crisis situations. Let's use the example of being chased by a tiger. Cortisol makes you breathe more rapidly, and your heart pound so you can run fast. Cortisol does this by directing increased blood flow toward your heart and lungs and away from less necessary systems in the moment, like your digestive system, reproductive system, hands, and feet. You don't need to feel discomfort in your feet while running from a tiger: You just need to run. You don't focus on eating well while running from a tiger—again, just run!

What if you can't outrun the tiger and you can't beat it in combat? The cortisol in your body encourages you to freeze and play dead. Maybe the tiger will leave you alone if it thinks you're long dead and not good to eat. Your breathing slows down and becomes so shallow it's almost like you're not breathing at all. You still don't feel your hands and feet, which might have gone cold, because your body knows it's best not to feel pain if

"When you have PTSD, your brain has made connections necessary for survival."

you're being eaten. The problem with living in this state is this: If you're constantly in dangerous situations, the parts of your body that don't get enough blood flow might start to become imbalanced, and the tissue may break down, as will the parts that get too much blood flow. This creates health problems for those areas.

But who is being chased by a tiger, anyway? Not us! But unfortunately, the human body doesn't know the difference between stress as a response to a tiger or a scary voice mail. And if you are stuck in a constant loop of trauma or unresolved traumatic experiences, your body will continue to take damage as it stays in this cortisol-induced survival mode. This is particularly harsh on teens because your body is already doing so much growing and changing. Increased cortisol from PTSD can damage your tissues and contribute to longer-term health challenges. This is another reason to address PTSD—so you can help your body go back to its relaxed state and function properly.

> "The human body doesn't know the difference between stress as a response to a tiger or a scary voice mail."

[Roz's Story]

Roz didn't realize their childhood was abusive or neglectful. All they knew was that their mother always rejected or criticized every little thing they did, and their father was angry and unpredictable when he was around. Their parents took pride in never cursing at them, but Roz couldn't count how many times their family made them feel worthless. Roz often felt alone at home—their parents and brother were either out working or doing other activities, and when they were home, they made it clear they had no interest in spending time with Roz.

Roz felt isolated even at school. They were friendly with most people, but there was seldom anyone Roz felt really close to. Sometimes Roz wished they had people they were close to, but often it didn't matter to them. Roz didn't realize this could be a symptom of depression. Roz also dealt with anxious symptoms without realizing it. Sometimes in class, for example, they would suddenly feel very exposed, like they had to zip up their jacket and be as inconspicuous as possible, even though they were dressed to blend in, and nobody was looking at them. Roz often felt very tired, no matter how much sleep they got, and their body often felt very sensitive—even if they bumped into something lightly, it could still hurt an hour later. It wasn't until they graduated from high school, moved away, and decided to try therapy that they learned they might be experiencing a form of PTSD.

PTSD SELF-EVALUATION

What are some of the symptoms you are experiencing? This self-evaluation can't diagnose you, but it can be a good starting point to getting the support you need. If you've already received a PTSD diagnosis, you can also use this tool to track how you are doing with healing and recovery. Put a check mark next to each statement that has been true for you in the past month.

☐ I've had upsetting memories of my traumatic experience pop into my head, even though I didn't want them to.

☐ I've had nightmares about my traumatic experience.

☐ I've suddenly felt like I was back in my traumatic experience, either experiencing the event all over again or experiencing the exact feelings I had at the time.

☐ I've gotten very emotional when something reminded me of what happened.

☐ My body has reacted to being reminded of what happened (muscles tightened, heart raced, breathing changed, stomach hurt, etc.).

☐ I've gone out of my way to avoid thoughts and feelings about the experience.

☐ I've avoided people, places, and things that could remind me of the experience.

☐ It's been hard to remember important parts of what happened, or the memories are fuzzy or in a mixed-up order.

☐ I've thought negatively about myself, other people, or the world as a whole.

- [ ] I've blamed myself for what happened to me.
- [ ] I've felt strong, negative emotions about what happened, which took over my mind for a while.
- [ ] I'm not interested in things I usually enjoy doing, including spending time with people I like.
- [ ] I've felt alone even when I was around other people.
- [ ] I've had difficulty feeling positive feelings.
- [ ] I've been on edge and had a short temper.
- [ ] I've self-harmed on purpose.
- [ ] I've felt very on guard, jumpy, or paranoid.
- [ ] It's been hard to pay attention.
- [ ] I've had trouble falling or staying asleep.
- [ ] I've felt like I wasn't real, the world around me wasn't real, or like I was watching myself from out of my body.

PTSD Self-Evaluation: Next Steps

It takes many symptoms to determine whether you have PTSD or another mental health condition. But whether you are experiencing PTSD or having a hard time because of any of these symptoms, it's worth talking to someone. I recommend finding a trusted professional. You can start by talking with a trusted adult in your school, at home, or in your community who can help you find the support you need. Also, please check out the resources on page 137 that offer help and guidance to teens in need.

Identifying Your Healing Barriers

Healing isn't always easy. Even at its simplest, you still need to examine the emotional and/or physical wounds, get the right treatments for what you are experiencing, and keep up with the healing process even when it's uncomfortable. In addition, everyone has a different experience and might not have the same kind of access to (or even the kind of home situation that encourages getting) help and healing. Not having enough money, a reliable source of transportation, or a caregiver available to help you, for example, may keep you from getting the support you need. These kinds of obstacles can become a healing barrier.

The good news is you can resolve some of these obstacles once you're aware of them. Some of them might be out of your hands. Just like the trauma you experience is not your fault nor in your control, sometimes there are parts of your potential success that you can't influence right now. It's important to take stock of what you can do and what you cannot, then treat yourself kindly as you do your best. Humans are amazingly resilient, even when conditions are not ideal.

First, identify your physical or emotional injury and examine it truthfully. If you are still experiencing active trauma, it might not be safe or convenient for you to seek help for what you are experiencing. If so, this is a barrier to healing right now, but the primary goal in this case is to work toward establishing immediate safety and stability. You might also struggle with being honest with yourself about whether you need support. A lot of people mistakenly believe that being "strong" means not being affected by anything and finding a way to win no matter what. Many research studies show that this kind of thinking only leads to worsened anxiety, depression, and health consequences in the long term. You might worry that others will think you are strange or "crazy" for feeling the way you do. There are reasons you feel the way you do. Feelings might not always be accurate, but they are valid and worth respecting. If your experience is getting in the way of a life that works best for you, it's worth seeking support.

The second area of possible barriers is getting the right treatments and support for what you're experiencing. There are several reasons for this. It may be hard to find therapists who are affordable and offer the kind of treatment that works best for you. Your friends, family, and even parts of your community might discourage you from seeking help. If this is the

> **"**Healing also means dedicating time and energy to dealing with your experience.**"**

case, you might choose to reconsider your beliefs and what you've been taught so you can seek out people who support your needs. You may have challenges finding reliable transportation or fitting treatment into your schedule. Even spending time reading this book has required you to spend resources, and not everyone has that option. Finally, although I wish all therapists were amazing and perfect for everyone, that's just not true. Therapists are as varied as any other part of humanity. It's important to feel connected to the person you work with. Unfortunately, sometimes we just don't click, but finding someone you do click with is a vital step to getting the relief and help you need.

The third area in which you might find barriers to your healing is keeping up the process even when it feels uncomfortable. Treatment for PTSD is uncomfortable because, instead of trying to hide it all away, treatment means telling the story, feeling the feelings, and finding a way to process it all as best we can. Wouldn't everyone love to avoid having to think about and feel any of that and still come out perfectly healed? Yes, please! But the only way you can really heal is by dealing with what happened and your current challenges head-on; otherwise, it sticks around, half-buried, and gets more complicated the longer you wait.

Healing also means dedicating time and energy to dealing with your experience, even as the rest of the world continues forward. This process isn't convenient, and not everything or everyone in your life will respect that you've made your healing and growth a priority. You might feel pressure to just "get over it" and get back to pretending everything is fine and normal because it makes *other* people more comfortable. You might even feel temporary comfort in staying busy and not thinking about your needs. Because of this, it can be tempting to put off and avoid the work now, even if it means having a harder time later in life. Unfortunately, the unresolved issue will wait for you and get harder and more demanding as time goes on, so putting in the effort now is worth it. If it was easy and you could just snap your fingers and have it be gone with no trace, it wouldn't have affected you the way it did. PTSD hits you hard because it *is* hard.

EXERCISE

Now that we've discussed some possible healing barriers, take a moment and see if you can identify what barriers you might face. Keep in mind that some obstacles can become a step to resolve and conquer, but others might just be something to accept and give your best effort. What barriers might you face:

Recognizing your struggles and needs with honesty and compassion?

_____

_____

_____

Getting the treatment and support you need for healing?

_____

_____

_____

Continuing to work on your healing process over time, even when it's uncomfortable or inconvenient?

_____

_____

_____

EXERCISE

PTSD keeps us stuck on our trauma and disconnects us from ourselves and the present life going on around us. Reconnecting with the present is one way to help yourself recover. Let's try a reconnecting exercise. Take a moment to settle into your body. Don't try to change anything—just notice what's happening inside you. What area feels the warmest in your body right now? The coldest? What muscles are the tensest? Most relaxed? Are there any parts of your body that feel numb, tingly, or like they've dropped out of existence? Just notice for now and write down any observations.

_____

_____

_____

_____

_____

_____

_____

_____

_____

_____

_____

_____

CLOSING CHECK-IN

You've made it to the end of the first and biggest chapter! Whether you're here because you read straight through, or you felt like you needed a check-in, great job—you're here either way. Take a moment to just breathe and be honest about what it's like to read about trauma and maybe even revisit your own. Maybe you're doing fine with all this information. Or maybe you're having a tough time right now. You might feel somewhere in between. There is no judgment; each human experience is unique. What do you need in this moment? A good stretch, a walk around, or maybe a snack? Maybe there's a song you'd like to listen to while you think about how you feel. Maybe it's time for some fresh air, a drink of water, or some interpretive dance to work out any pent-up energy.

You might want to pause working in this workbook and do something else for the rest of the day or until you can talk with a mental health professional. If you feel very upset about anything you've read here or about your own experience, a helpful thing to do while you wait to talk to a therapist is to write it out. Even if you don't have a therapist, journaling is still a great way to process your experience. You can also try recording your thoughts in audio or video. Putting your feelings and thoughts into words can help you feel more at ease, as it quiets the nerves and emotions enough for the processing part of your brain to work.

This is a good time to think back on what you've learned here. Maybe some of it was new, and maybe some of it you already knew. Maybe you read something here that immediately clicked for you and put words to an experience you've had for some time now. On the other side of that possibility, maybe something didn't make sense. Maybe there's something you felt was missing. Whatever your experience, this is your book to use how you want. Feel free to go back and jot notes, questions, or doodles next to parts that need them. You can always come back and read any part of this chapter over again.

So, take a slow, deep breath and sigh it out. Get a good stretch. Wiggle your limbs a bit and shake them out. Get a glass of water. Look at something cute. Healing isn't something that happens in one big chunk all at once—it starts slowly, one piece at a time. Being honest about your feelings and what you need is a fantastic way to start.

Key Takeaways

You covered a lot of general information about PTSD in this chapter. You learned about the history of the disorder, how it could affect you as a teenager, some of the obstacles you may face in your healing, and how you might handle them.

- People have experienced symptoms of post-traumatic stress disorder since early times, but it wasn't until the Vietnam War that we called it "PTSD." We now understand the disorder to affect people who experience all types of traumas.

- There are many types of potentially traumatic events. You might experience a single event or a lifetime of traumas stacked together. Regardless, your trauma is as valid as anyone else's. If you experienced something that changed how you think of yourself, others, and the world around you, you've experienced trauma. Anyone who was traumatized deserves the appropriate support and healing.

- Your teenage years are important for growth and development. PTSD, especially during this time, comes with serious mental, emotional, and physical effects that can last into adulthood. Treatment is important and valid, no matter how many symptoms you do or do not have.

- There might be internal and/or external obstacles to your healing process. Some of them are things you can think through and overcome. Others may be out of your hands for now. Do what you can and be gentle with yourself. Every bit of healing counts.

The chapters ahead will give you a closer look at the kinds of work you might do as you heal. You'll be able to use the exercises and activities ahead to practice calming your nervous system and connecting yourself to your present experience, getting yourself unstuck from the past. You will also find opportunities to express what you went through, which can help you feel more in charge of your own experience.

Another part of your safety and stability comes from taking care of your basic needs. Before you move on, and whenever you choose to pick up this book, consider whether you are in a safe frame of mind to get into some potentially difficult topics. If you are already feeling tired, hungry, or stressed out, the same information that can help you one day might feel overwhelming the next. When this happens, take care of yourself. Nourish your body, hydrate, get rested, take prescribed medications, and get some movement in, even if it's a short dance party or walk by yourself. This book will be here when you get back.

Working through Your Trauma

Welcome to chapter 2, where you'll find valuable exercises aimed to help you through PTSD. The understanding you have is a great first step toward healing; now it's time to put what you learn into practice. Every time you practice something new, your brain grows new connections between the neurons. These "neuronal connections" make it easier to do that new thing again in the future. That's also why it can be hard to get out of old habits and survival responses—because those connections are so established and powerful, it's easier to do those things. But if you work at it, you can change what comes easy to you.

These activity-rich chapters are here to guide you in doing new things and building new directions for yourself. Some might be difficult or feel awkward at first but will likely get better the more you practice. It's a big ask; I get it—you aren't often asked to look at your own thoughts and feelings and take them apart to rearrange them! Just know the work you do will pay off in the long run.

This chapter will help you identify how your trauma affects you specifically and what you can do about it. Your experience with each of your symptoms can and will change over time, so definitely revisit these topics and activities in the future. Doing so will help you address the symptoms you experience even as they change, and you'll notice your own growth and healing along the way.

Before we get into the specifics of activities for change, we'll talk about a few challenges you might experience along the way (it's worth knowing what you're getting into before you get into it). Then we'll talk about some of the trickier parts of PTSD to manage, like triggers that cause flashbacks and panic attacks, intrusive thoughts, and emotional dysregulation. Once you learn about the difficulties that affect your healing, you'll discover different ways of managing them.

Following is a list of the main topics we'll cover. As always, feel free to pick and choose what you want to read first and when you want to read it. Mark off the topics as you go along, or mark which ones you want to come back to again. Make notes, doodles, and write questions wherever you'd like to:

☐ Why PTSD Can Be Hard to Work Through

☐ Triggers: What They Are & How to Manage Them

☐ Banishing Intrusive Thoughts

☐ Unpacking Your Emotions

[Ivan's Story]

Ivan was terrified driving home from a long trip at the beginning of the summer. He'd gotten caught in a storm and had a hard time seeing as he drove. It was difficult to stay awake on the road for so long, but every motel he passed said "No Vacancy." He had taken caffeine pills and another stimulant to keep him awake, but the resulting spike in adrenaline and cortisol pushed him into terror. His eyes were blurry, and his heart was pounding. "No Vacancy." "No Vacancy." He wished he hadn't gone so far from home. There were so many moments when he was scared his car would crash. Completely panicked, all he could do was keep driving.

Ivan made it home safely and tried to push the bad experience out of his mind. But for the next day and every day after that, there would be a moment or two where he would flash back to when he was terrified on the road. "No Vacancy." He felt sick to his stomach every time, and his heart pounded. He pushed the thoughts and feelings away, telling himself he would probably feel better near the end of the summer and didn't mention it to anybody. But, as school started again, the flashbacks continued. Ivan decided to go to the school counselor's office and tell them what he was experiencing. The counselor explained he could be experiencing a form of PTSD. Ivan found that talking about his experience and learning to relax around it helped tremendously.

Why PTSD Can Be Hard to Work Through

Let's be honest: PTSD is hard to work through, and some aspects of being a teenager can make it more challenging. One of those challenges is being in environments you can't control, like school, social events, and even home. So, you might not have the option to take extra time when you want to just chill and focus on healing. You might have tons of homework, an after-school job, extracurricular activities, or college applications to complete. There is real pressure to do well and achieve as much as possible in any of these situations. So many teens are pressured to do well in the world and be competitive in many ways: in school, sports, skills, hobbies, work, and socially, to name a few. This is a tough time in life where schedules are often packed tight, and you're also figuring out who you want to be in the world. You may wonder about what the world will hold for you. Balancing responsibilities on top of this uncertainty isn't easy.

And here you are, trying to be okay after something traumatic. I commend your courage and want you to know that what you're doing with your life right now, in working on healing, is much more important than school pressures. At the same time, I understand that not participating in school pressure isn't an option for most kids. But for you, that means making time for yourself and your mental health even more important. What if your needs were nonnegotiable? What kinds of supports does your school offer for someone who needs them? What are the obstacles to you making time for yourself? Those obstacles are a "to-do list" of things to handle so you can be well.

Expectations and schedules are a part of social life, too. The way you manage friendships and relationships now will help you determine who and how you want to be around others in the future. But social life means other people, and other people aren't always dedicated to our well-being. You might have to set boundaries about conversations you're willing to be a part of and activities you do and don't want to participate in. Gossip or rumors about not only what you've been through—but also what others

"What if your needs were nonnegotiable?"

might be going through—can be harmful. It's perfectly fine to say, "I don't want to talk about that. I'd appreciate it if you didn't, either," "I think it's disrespectful to talk about other people like that," or "I'm going to walk away from any conversation about that." Hopefully, others respect your wishes, but the real boundary solidifies when they do it anyway, and you follow through on what you said you would do.

The same goes for things like drinking or using drugs. Substance use is a form of detaching from your present and generally signals to your brain that you are not safe. Your brain has its own mechanisms of disengaging when you are not safe, so when you disengage on purpose, your brain processes the message that your environment was one you needed to escape from. This might make you feel more anxious in that setting in the future; you also will not fully process information in an altered state. This can delay or alter your healing process, as connection and processing are ideal for healing. Struggling with substance abuse is a common problem, especially during and after trauma. Regardless of the details of your struggles, you deserve to heal from your difficult experiences.

You have the right to set boundaries around what you do and don't want, even if you didn't set a boundary in the past. It is hard losing friends and people you care about because they don't respect you. However, your health and happiness are worth more than their disrespect, and you will free yourself to find new people who respect and appreciate you fully.

Home life can also be challenging, as it's another area not entirely in your control. You may have supportive caregivers and family members who understand what you've been through and are there to help. Even then, each of those people continues to have their own lives, difficulties, and responsibilities, so they may not always be available to help. Unfortunately, home might also be an unstable and unpredictable place that isn't conducive to healing. In this case, you may need to work on what you can now and know that your healing will have to continue once you've moved out. The important thing is to understand what you can do to make your life as stable and safe as possible and do your best to manage the things you can't control or influence. Things outside your influence can be stressful, but pouring all your frustration into trying to change something you can't tends to make things worse.

The world is also chaotic. The news and even social media are full of unexpected and often upsetting things. We care about others, and it's hard to see suffering and negativity worldwide. It's important to care about things that matter, yet even caring has its limits. If you are constantly exposing yourself to upsetting events because it's important to you to care about them, you are likely to hit a point of feeling overwhelmed and overloaded that shuts you down from being able to help and support others. Staying in the know is valuable, but so is knowing your limit. It can be a true act of self-care to unplug for a while. When you choose to return, find sources of information that feel less harmful, and empower yourself by putting your care into action through kind words or volunteering your skills.

EXERCISE

Sharing your experience with people you trust will help you process the traumatic event and heal. However, you do not owe every person every detail of your story—your experience and healing process belong to you. Some people may also not be ready to hear every detail. Consider practicing how you want to talk about your experience. What do you want to share so you feel most empowered and in control of your own narrative? How might you start the conversation with a friend? How do you want to talk about your challenges? Pretend you are someone reacting to your story with uncomfortable questions. How might you answer to protect your privacy?

_____

_____

_____

_____

_____

_____

_____

_____

_____

_____

_____

_____

[Laura's Story]

All Laura had to do was think about it, and her mind would reexperience the car crash she was in. Her brother was driving their car when another car turned right in front of them. Thankfully, everyone made it out okay other than a few scrapes and bruises. But, even months later, Laura's attention would slip back to the moment of impact, and she could feel the sensations of their car hitting the other. She also found herself worrying about whether her brother was safe, and she'd often check his location on her phone to make sure he wasn't in one place for too long. Then she would confront him, assuming he'd done something risky. Her brother expressed frustration that Laura was checking up on him. These arguments turned into more frequent fights. Laura's brother finally yelled, "You need help!" At the time, it made Laura angrier.

Once they made up, her brother brought up getting support more gently. He told her that living life scared wasn't living at all and that she deserved to move past the crash. She tearfully agreed to see a therapist. In therapy, she learned that her worries about her brother had become intrusive thoughts she pushed away by compulsively checking for his location and that this temporary relief kept her worries strong in the long term. She learned how to relax and feel safer during both her flashbacks and the intrusive thoughts, which soon diminished in frequency and severity.

Triggers: What They Are & How to Manage Them

People with PTSD can become emotionally and physically flooded when directly or vaguely reminded of the trauma experience. These reminders are what we call "triggers." "Being triggered" is not the same as being upset about something you've heard, read, or seen. With PTSD, triggers overwhelm your system and ability to stay present while you reexperience what happened or break down in a physical and psychological panic. This response happens because your nervous system is suddenly terrified for your survival and well-being. Because traumatic memories are fragmented and not processed adequately in PTSD, the brain doesn't always know what to do with all the pieces and parts when suddenly reminded of them.

Traumatic experiences are often confusing and come with a lot of complicated feelings. A trigger can cause you to suddenly feel the exact feelings you felt during your trauma, even in completely different surroundings. Panic attacks are strong physiological panic responses where your heart may race, and you may breathe heavily while experiencing strong chest pressure or even pain. It's common to mistake panic attacks for heart attacks, as chest pain and a sense of impending doom are common in both.

Triggers vary from person to person and depend on the traumatic experience. For example, if you were eating an apple when a violent and life-threatening event occurred, you may not be able to taste, smell, or look at an apple after the event without triggering overwhelming panic or reexperiencing that violent event. However, what the brain latches on to as a trigger isn't usually predictable. Some people may avoid engaging with others and doing things they enjoy to avoid any possible triggers of traumatic memories.

Two methods for managing triggers are exposure and response prevention (ERP) and acceptance and commitment therapy (ACT). In ERP, you practice techniques such as progressive muscle relaxation, deep breathing, and other ways of encouraging feelings of calm and peace within yourself. You make a list of triggers and rank them from low to high. Then, slowly and mindfully, you practice relaxation techniques while exposing yourself first to the smallest triggers that cause only a little bit of distress, before working your way up the list.

ACT is kind of the same idea. In ACT, you learn that people think thoughts all the time and will have memories all the time, but the more you can let go of the pressure, judgment, and emotions attached to those thoughts and memories, the less they bother you. You allow the thoughts and feelings to come and go as they please. Your job is to acknowledge they are there, not attach meaning or emotion to them, and refocus back on your goals and values. These explanations are not a full instruction manual on ERP or ACT, but the techniques we'll explore later in this chapter are inspired by these practices.

The point of both kinds of treatments, which can be done together, is to help the brain associate upsetting and triggering things with calm, relaxation, and nonchalance. Avoiding triggers can be helpful at first—the brain is warning you about things associated with your trauma in hopes that you will avoid further harm and traumatic experience. If you had a bad medical experience because you got bit by a scorpion, for example, it's a good idea to avoid scorpions. But when your triggers become things like apples, hanging out with your friends, doing art, or functioning in everyday life, avoiding these triggers becomes limiting and disruptive. With that, your brain gets stronger at enforcing those trigger reactions. It can become difficult to leave the house or even your room as you try to avoid triggers, and the effects of PTSD grow stronger.

Working to de-trigger your triggers is uncomfortable but important work. It frees you to enjoy your life and do everything you need to do every day. It keeps you from being trapped under the limitations of fear and worry that you will have a panic attack or reexperience your trauma. That doesn't mean you should go out and start looking for every single trigger to try and conquer immediately! Your body is focused on keeping you safe while it struggles to process overwhelming information about what you've already been through. It's important to take your time and build your sense of safety and stability first. When you try to power too quickly and too hard through triggering material, you can experience re-traumatization because you are not yet prepared to handle such strong experiences. It is easy to feel impatient about healing when you've already been through so much. Going slow but doing it safely and thoroughly is better than going fast and experiencing more pain and trauma. You are worth taking the time for.

"You are worth taking the time for."

EXERCISE

Memory functions strangely during trauma. The human brain has a difficult time encoding this chaotic information and, as a result, can end up with weird fragments, haziness, or changing memories about what happened. There might also be parts you don't remember at all, even though you were there. If you feel safe to do so right now, take a breath and settle into your body. What pieces of the trauma stand out to you? What's hard to remember? How has this changed over time? You can write about it or draw some pictures to reflect on this activity, then revisit this exercise later in your healing and compare.

EXERCISE

What triggers do you experience for your trauma? When you feel comfortable doing so, make a list ranking some triggers from 1 (just bugs you a little) to 10 (is completely overwhelming). Starting with one of the easiest items, ranked as a 1, think about how you can take this back for yourself. What is something you would rather associate that trigger with? Prior to the trauma, did this trigger remind you of something pleasant? How do you want to feel when you encounter it? Practice stretching and relaxing your muscles as you consider a new connection. Practice this response and, over time, it will stick. As you master the lower-ranked triggers, you'll build the skills needed to carefully practice again with increasingly strong triggers.

1. _____

2. _____

3. _____

4. _____

5. _____

6. _____

7. _____

8. _____

9. _____

10. _____

MIDWAY CHECK-IN

Let's check in. How do you feel about how much you've just read? Sometimes the brain feels overloaded when you try to process complicated or vast information. You can learn and understand better, though, by explaining the information to other people. Try writing a letter or making a recording as if you were talking to a friend, a pet, or even a fictional character. You don't have to actually send it to them—this is just for you. How would you explain to them what you've learned? What stuck out for you, and what are you still unsure about? Was anything just outright confusing? Are there examples you can give that would help them understand better? Does any part of what you learned remind you of something from a movie, a show, or something online? How does the information connect with your own experience, or how might it be different? When you can connect examples to information and find different ways to explain it, you're likely to understand it even better.

Once you've given this check-in exercise a shot, take a moment to feel out your current energy. Are you ready to read more, review what you've already read, or stop for now? Honor what you need.

Banishing Intrusive Thoughts

Intrusive thoughts can drive you up the wall. They are things you don't want to think about, but they seem to force their way in and make you feel really upset. Intrusive thoughts may pop into your head because of a trigger, and they can come up more spontaneously the more often you try to shut them out completely. These thoughts could be about bad things happening to you or others. They could be thoughts about doing harmful or dangerous things. They could be negative statements, like "I am worthless." You feel stuck trying to avoid these upsetting ideas, but the harder you fight them, the stronger they seem to be!

Intrusive thoughts form because there is a topic you care very strongly about, and because you are so upset at just the thought of that idea, you bully yourself about it. The more you bully yourself and try to stop thinking the intrusive thought, the more psychological pressure you put on yourself. Your brain notices that psychological pressure and interprets it like this: "Oh! This must be an important topic and is probably really dangerous because this person is so upset. They should think about it even more often and feel even more uncomfortable about it because clearly, this is important to always check for."

The brain's reaction to intrusive thoughts is a lot like the body's reaction to an allergen. For example, pollen likely isn't going to kill you, but your immune system might be so strong that it will throw an absolute fit unless you take medicine that helps it relax. Similarly, just thinking something isn't going to hurt you or other people, but your strong mental security system is so strong, it's locking down every time the thought comes up. It's doing its best to protect you and others, even if you don't really need that protection.

But the truth is, everyone has thoughts about all kinds of things all the time: positive, negative, neutral. The difference is, when most people have a thought they don't want, they brush it off without worrying about it. For people with intrusive thoughts, however, you instead start worrying about why you are thinking those things and about how awful it would be if it were true. Then you try to stuff away the thought and the associated uncomfortable feelings. But the harder you push, the harder these things push back. Next thing you know, you're stuck in a mental prison where you're constantly feeling tense and worried about what you're thinking about. It's exhausting.

> **"You are defined by your actions more than your thoughts."**

It's important to remind yourself that you are defined by your actions more than your thoughts. For example, thinking about doing community service all the time doesn't count as volunteering. The same goes for negative intrusive thoughts. Your brain can imagine all kinds of things, but what matters most is what really happens and how you respond. Say you're worried about whether you will be successful in the future. Instead of pushing the worry down, take the opportunity to think, write out, or talk to a friend about it. Maybe you'll find just by talking about it, the power of the worry goes away. Or maybe there are some steps you can take to nudge things in a good direction. In the case of worrying about your future, you might choose to learn more about a subject you're interested in or write a letter to someone in that career to ask questions.

Once you've reflected on the concerns an intrusive thought brings up, it's time to practice taking the power away. The more you respond to a thought like it's not intrusive, like it's no big deal, the more your brain will respond until that becomes true. Where do you feel tension in your body when the intrusive thoughts come up? Practice relaxing those areas. As disturbing as intrusive thoughts can be, you really can get better over time with a "fake it 'til you make it" approach. When you respond with calm to intrusive thoughts, your brain notices and says, "Oh, this must not be as big of a deal as I thought it was. I'll check in on it less often and with less alarm." Intrusive thoughts seldom get better the first time you practice this, but it really makes a difference over time.

Remember that you have intrusive thoughts because your brain is trying to be protective. You are also more likely to have intrusive thoughts when you are already vulnerable because you are tired, hungry, stressed, etc. As you do the work to get past intrusive thoughts, also notice if they are a sign you need to take care of your body. Are you tired? Hungry? Stressed? If so, it's perfectly okay to avoid the thoughts just for now so you can handle those needs. Don't forget, decent people like you have all kinds of wild thoughts throughout their daily life, but they know which ones deserve attention and which do not. You are not the things you think.

EXERCISE

One way to depower intrusive thoughts is to practice acting calm and relaxed, like this is any other thought you might have. Here's a goofy example: If a dog wore pants, how would they look? Would they cover just the back legs? The butt? All the legs? All the legs and the butt? Thinking about dog pants, notice how it feels to laugh, shrug, and brush it off. Remember this feeling and practice it. The next time you have an intrusive thought, try treating it like thinking about dog pants. The more you practice calm and consistently label the thought as unimportant, the less upsetting it'll become. Write your ideas below.

_____

_____

_____

_____

_____

_____

_____

_____

_____

_____

MIDWAY CHECK-IN

Digging into your thoughts can be unsettling, because you haven't necessarily made a habit yet of examining your mental patterns so closely. Take a moment to check in with yourself and see how you're feeling. You might feel good about what you've learned and the exercises you've done. You might also feel burned out or even emotionally upset after having to revisit your own trauma and challenging thoughts. This is a very normal sign that you've touched on something important and should slow down to give it attention. What would feel nice and supportive right now? Is it lying in the grass outside, talking to a friend, or meditating? Is it time for a bit of kickboxing or a yell into your pillow? Take the kind of break you need for yourself.

Your brain learns from everything you do, big and small. That means even small changes you make today, like reading this book and maybe doing one exercise, will make a difference in the long run. Don't worry about "not doing enough." The most important thing is that you do what works best for you. Your "enough" is awesome. It's okay to want to be able to do more. That ability, as with anything, will come with time and practice. Do just enough today and leave some energy for yourself to enjoy your day.

[*Miguel's Story*]

It was hard enough for Miguel to tell his parents and those close to him that he had been sexually assaulted. He knew that telling was the right thing to do, because keeping it to himself wasn't fair to him and could also put other people at risk if the assaulter wasn't reported. But once he shared his story, he started facing questions he didn't feel comfortable answering or wasn't ready for. Some people questioned his experience or made disparaging remarks about his gender or sexuality. Some made nasty comments about how they would have "avoided" the situation. But the thing was, they *hadn't* been in his situation, and Miguel felt angry at the judgment and blame he faced. What he went through wasn't his fault!

All the while, Miguel battled with feeling scared or closed off around friends and others at school. He had panic attacks in class, and sometimes the smell of certain people or hearing certain songs would trigger emotional and mental flashbacks. He began to wish he could stay in his room and avoid everyone for the rest of his life. It was hard to ask for help when he was in the middle of the swirls of emotions and thoughts PTSD brought his way, but he communicated to his parents the best he could, once he realized what he was going through. He and his parents were able to find a therapist who specialized in trauma and helped Miguel get unstuck from his triggers and challenging emotions.

Unpacking Your Emotions

The survival-focused disorganization of PTSD means that your feelings can become unpredictable. You may burst into tears about what happened even though you are in the middle of something completely calm. You may not feel happy about something you usually really enjoy. You may feel angry and unsure about why you are so irritated. You may feel numb to everything. Emotional processing is not at its best under PTSD, not unlike how memories can feel like a mess following trauma. You now know that if you try to push the negative feelings away, they get more pressurized and pop back up harder or at even more unlikely times. If you let every emotion run your life, your actions and environment can become as disorganized as those feelings.

Balance is the goal. It's not easy to achieve, and it can be different for everyone, but it's important to figure out the right amount and kinds of emotional expression for you. Part of this is also figuring out what the emotions are related to. For example, if you have an emotional flashback, a small part of the feelings you experience could be directly related to the present, but most of the feelings are likely about the trauma you experienced. Emotions are one language through which our brains communicate information. Feeling irritated, for example, can be communicating "I don't like this." Part of finding emotional balance is learning to interpret what the messages are, figuring out where the messages belong, and learning to handle them in the right way.

A common phenomenon following trauma is called "emotional incongruity." This is when someone talks about awful things that happened but does it while smiling, laughing, or using a muted response. This is a coping mechanism signaling that what happened is so heavy emotionally, the brain has chosen to disconnect from the negativity of the trauma to try and protect the person. People might say, "I have to laugh about it, otherwise I'll cry," or "that's just my sense of humor." I've also heard "I'm afraid if I let myself cry, I'll never stop," or "if I express my anger, I worry I will just keep going until everything is destroyed." I respect that everyone does what they can to cope in their own way. It's also important to

> "Emotions are one language through which our brains communicate information."

recognize this as a sign of deep hurts and trauma still inside. It's your choice to decide if you'll continue to carry it; just know you don't have to. It's uncomfortable work, but the ability to cry about something and then be okay is possible and worthwhile.

Regardless of the emotions and how they pop up, "unpacking them" means thinking through them and finding healthy ways to express them. Emotions are information: Their reason for being is to communicate and be understood. Once you have allowed your emotions to communicate in an appropriate way, they often move forward instead of keeping you stuck. So, when an emotion pops up, the first goal is to notice it and label it. This keeps you from being stuck inside it, because you have to be able to take a step back to examine it so you can recognize and say, "I am feeling angry," for example.

Once you've labeled it, consider whether you are in a good time and place to unpack it. You might be in the middle of class, work, or a conversation with someone. Take note of that and figure out a time to process that feeling in more depth. You might have to accept that you could feel that feeling until you can process it later. It's entirely possible and okay to feel anxious and still do what you have to do.

When you have time to process that feeling, choose a method of expression that works best for you. This could look like journaling and writing out all the thoughts that come with the feeling until you feel like it has spoken its piece. You might want to make a video doing the same sort of thing. Once the words sort themselves out and the emotion feels like it's untied itself, you may have a clear sense of something you want to do for yourself. You might be able to establish a boundary with someone. You might realize you've been overworking yourself. Or it could be as simple as acknowledging that your trauma is still bothering you.

If you're not in a place to dissect a feeling like this, there are still things you can do. Anger, for example, is a feeling that often wants action before it's ready to resolve. If you feel angry and want to break something, you can try throwing ice on the sidewalk. If you struggle with self-harm urges, squeezing ice in your hand can also be helpful because the brain accepts the discomfort as if you had self-harmed even though you are safe. You can also try holding your hands open and down at your sides or palms-up on your lap. Because this is the opposite of balling your fists up, which the body often wants to do when we're angry, it communicates to your brain that maybe you aren't so angry after all and that you can let yourself feel a little more at peace.

EXERCISE

Now that you've learned about unpacking your emotions, why not try a meditation exercise that can help? Get comfortable and close your eyes, or gaze softly at the floor in front of you. Mentally label each inhalation "breathing in" and each exhalation "breathing out." If any feelings come up, label those, too: "happy," "sad," "annoyed," "bored," or whatever they are. When you get distracted, which we all do, just label it "distraction" and go back to your breathing. Keep practicing, and you will get better at noticing and naming feelings instead of feeling stuck inside them. How did this exercise go?

_____

_____

_____

_____

_____

_____

_____

_____

_____

_____

_____

_____

_____

CLOSING CHECK-IN

It's time to check in with yourself. You've navigated this chapter and learned about your triggers, intrusive thoughts, and how to try and wrangle emotions that might feel all over the place. This work can be exhausting, especially when you're first getting started. How are you feeling in this moment? Get a good stretch, shake out your limbs, high-five yourself (you deserve it!), and make sure to hydrate. Take a moment and a few deep breaths, sighing out the air at the end. Is any part of your body feeling numb, tingly, or fuzzy? Sometimes bodies "disconnect" like this when they're overwhelmed. Maybe your brain just feels like overly warm mush. That's another sign that you've done more than enough today.

Working to unravel complicated thoughts and feelings can take a big emotional toll, and this isn't something to take lightly. If you're struggling to get through this content and the exercises, please focus on your physical and emotional needs. It is hard to press toward emotional growth when you're hungry, exhausted, or generally stressed out by other things. As we discussed in the section about triggers, uncomfortable thoughts and feelings tend to spring up more when you're already vulnerable—your brain will go out of the way to protect you even more and make those thoughts and feelings louder. PTSD keeps your mind and body disconnected from your present experience and forward growth. Focusing on what your difficulties "mean" and what you truly need in the moment helps tremendously with healing.

Take some time to be present. What's the weather like today? Do you have some soft blankets you could wrap around yourself or an animal in your life who might need petting right now? Wiggle your toes for a few seconds, and just focus all your attention on how that feels. Being present can be uncomfortable sometimes, but it can also be pleasant. Being in the moment and taking a break from thoughts can help bring you a sense of peace. The more you get used to peace, the easier it is to find, even when things are stressful around you. And if your present moment is uncomfortable? This is temporary and will eventually become something else, whether neutral or even joyful. Just focusing on the discomfort and breathing through it can also be a peaceful experience, as your brain gets the signal to relax rather than distract. Be here. Your "here" will get better.

Key Takeaways

Chapter 2 is done! You took what you've learned and put in some of your own work. That probably came with a taste of how difficult this process can feel, but it gets easier the more you practice. You've already started growing neuronal connections in the direction of healing. Amazing. Let's review what you've learned.

- Working through PTSD can be hard for reasons that have nothing to do with you other than age. You can't control the people around you, and you're probably under academic and other pressures you can't change. This may also be a difficult time socially, as you figure out which friends respect your needs and boundaries and which you are better off letting go of. Hopefully, your home life is supportive, but even if it is, there may be other challenges your family has to focus on as well. These challenges make it even more important to prioritize what you need. Despite the obstacles, your well-being is valuable, and some healing is still better than none.

- Triggers are one serious way your brain tries to protect you after a difficult and traumatic event. By experiencing flashbacks and emotional spikes in response to harmless or even positive things, you may avoid situations your brain thinks of as dangerous. The reasoning makes sense, but the effect often limits your daily options. Rather than avoiding all triggers forever (which is impossible), the goal is to build your internal sense of peace and safety and then slowly confront your triggers one at a time, like you did on page 38. Although this work is uncomfortable, the decisions that help you expand your life and your options over time are generally healthier than those that make you shrink.

- Intrusive thoughts are a sign that you care deeply about the topic at hand. They also show that you worry about your own behavior and what may happen to others. The typical human response is to fight uncomfortable thoughts, but your brain responds to this by bringing the thoughts up more often and with stronger emotions. The result can feel like you're a prisoner in your own head. The solution is to relax into these uncomfortable moments, shrug them off the best you can, and refocus on your current goals. Over time, your brain learns there are more important and valuable things to focus on.

The next chapters will expand on what you have learned here and give you more tools to build the healing and growth you need, inside and out. When you're ready, let's move forward into processing your trauma.

Healing & Processing Your Trauma

Welcome to chapter 3! You learned about the background and general workings of PTSD in chapter 1. Chapter 2 brought you closer to your own experiences and helped you learn more about the specific challenges you may face, including triggers and intrusive thoughts. Now it's time to get into the work of untangling the difficult details of your experience. However, before we get into the tough work, we'll take some time to make sure you have a safe and stable environment to process in. You'll learn about the importance of having safe spaces for your healing and some ideas for making that for yourself.

Before we get going, take a moment to think about where you are in your own process. You do not have to resolve all your triggers to read this chapter and work on these exercises. If you feel like you're having trouble with this chapter because of intrusive thoughts or triggers, however, that's a good reason to slow down and just focus on working through those. Also, because trauma is messy, healing has to focus on what comes up, even if it seems disorganized. You may feel great about moving forward and doing really well, but then hit what feels like a roadblock that sends you back. This is normal and okay. Just notice where you are and what you need to do at the present time. This book will be here for you whenever and wherever you are in the process.

In this chapter, you'll explore the story that trauma tells you about yourself and how to take back the narrative. Then you'll consider your personal needs throughout the day and the tools you have to manage them. Finally, you'll read about having a strong support system, how to find the right people, and how to set up healthy communication and acceptance to keep it going.

Listed below are the main topics we will cover in this chapter. Feel free to flip through and read them in the order that works best for you. Make notes and doodles, write your thoughts, and highlight and color whatever helps you. You can check these off as you go along, mark them to come back to later, or do anything you want. This is your book and your experience.

☐ Make Your Space a Sanctuary

☐ Rewriting Your Story

☐ Your Coping Method Tool Kit

☐ The Importance of a Strong Support System

case study:

[Noura's Story]

Noura still remembers the night soldiers broke into her home. After that, her family fled their home and settled in a new country as refugees. Noura's heart ached for the friends and extended family she had to leave behind. At the same time, nightmares of the break-in still haunted her. It was hard for her to focus on learning in a new school when images of violence flashed in her head. And some people said nasty things about refugees. Her family's new life in this new country seemed otherwise calm enough, but none of it mattered because of what she had experienced.

Noura's school put together a therapy group for its refugee students. It felt kind of nice to be around others who had been through something similar, but it seemed like nobody was ready to share. The group made small talk about things they missed from their original home countries and thoughts about their school. But then they began to rant about the nasty comments they had heard about refugees. Noura felt more connected, knowing the others felt similarly in some ways. In the heat of one of these conversations, Noura felt comfortable mentioning her own traumatic experience. It felt like a dam broke in the group as each member began to talk about their trauma as well, and the pressure Noura held began to drain away.

Make Your Space a Sanctuary

Let's make a sanctuary space so you can better process what you've been through and heal through difficult circumstances. If you jump straight into digging through traumatic experiences, but everything around and inside of you is chaotic, chances are things could feel even more difficult, upsetting, and harmful. There needs to be a sense of increased safety and stability for you to return to and take comfort. Does a clean space feel safe? How about quiet? Maybe private or personalized? Let's focus on this.

Look at the space where you sleep. Is it in order? I'm not here to nag you about chores, I promise. It's just that having a freshly made bed or sleeping area is nice to return to when you've had a rough day. Is there laundry you could take care of and separate? It's okay to not do it all at once and, instead, handle maybe one or two things whenever you look at it. If putting things away "properly" is too much right now, you can put your things somewhere out of the way—that absolutely counts, too.

Do you have floor space you can clear up? It doesn't have to be spotless, but it's easier to relax when you can walk through a room without accidentally stepping on or tripping over something. Even if all you do is scoot those things out of the way, you'll make room for yourself. Are there dishes to take to the kitchen area and trash to throw away? It's okay if it feels like there is too much to do; set a timer for just two or five minutes and do what you can. Small habits will keep your space nice over time and give you a sense of peace and space day after day. The space you clear for yourself is worth it.

Once you've cleared your space just enough, think about ways you can arrange your things and decorate your space to create a sense of calm and happiness. Is there a good place to put a journal or art supplies? The easier it is to see and reach expressive tools that help your healing, the more likely you will use them. Maybe your safe space could use music you like or nice-smelling things. Think also about the lighting and any way to adjust it to make you more comfortable. Maybe string lights would help. What is the sound like in your space? Is it quiet enough for you to focus on your needs? The goal is to make a space you can count on when you need it.

If you share your space with someone, consider talking to them about how they can support you while acknowledging and respecting that this place also belongs to them. Mutual expectations about keeping things tidy,

> **"You get to decide what is special to you, and what matters is that it works for you."**

for example, are good to discuss. Maybe you don't have a lot of private space normally, but you can make a corner of the room or even a closet work for you. Could you hang up string lights or pretty cloth to make it feel cozier? Is there a study in the house you can use or a space outside somewhere? Even a tree you like to sit under can make all the difference. If there are no permanent spaces available to you, consider whether you can create a portable sanctuary. Is your space something you can take with you in a bag, with some items that help you feel peaceful and allow you to write out your feelings? Your space availability doesn't have to be perfect or fancy to work for you. You get to decide what is special to you, and what matters is that it works for you.

Another aspect of making something special and safe is time. Whether you have a space already, you can also decide that a specific time is safe for you. Maybe it's quiet right after you get home, and you can use that time for yourself. Maybe getting up in the morning gives you some time to yourself. You can take whatever moment works for you and dedicate it to your peace. It can also be worth it to talk to the people you live with about what times you can expect to have privacy or, at least, minimal disruption.

Once you've figured out what spaces and times work best for you, keep it as consistent as possible. As much as we may not think we like structure and routine, our minds and bodies thrive on structure. Having a predictable schedule and environment means you will be okay even on your worst days: Everything else can fall apart, but you'll still have your room, quiet times, and daily care routines to keep things together.

As with anything, making your time and space a sanctuary doesn't have to be perfect to be helpful. Every moment you take in a space that feels secure is another moment you add to your health and well-being. Do your best, take the time you need to get things set up, and make it a priority to keep your time and space feeling good for you. Whatever you can put together, your brain will experience that much more relief against the unpredictability and confusion you experienced through your trauma.

EXERCISE

We've discussed making a realistic sanctuary space based on what's available to you now, but that doesn't mean your dream location can't play a role. Take a moment and close your eyes or gaze softly at the floor. With no limitations, how would you imagine your perfect sanctuary space? What does it look like, sound like, smell like, feel like? What do you do in that space? Awesome. Now, what are creative ways you can bring those dreams into the space you have? Just because you don't live near the beach, for example, doesn't mean you can't decorate with a beach motif!

_____

_____

_____

_____

_____

_____

_____

_____

_____

_____

_____

[Lydia's Story]

One of the first things Lydia's therapist taught her was the importance of having a safe and stable space for unwinding and processing her thoughts. It made sense; the idea of talking about her traumatic experience felt scary enough without a sense of security already established. But home was one of the places where Lydia felt the unexpected could happen. Her little sister had health concerns and would sometimes need to be taken to the hospital in the middle of the day. The rest of the family often felt on edge and unsure when the next emergency would happen.

Lydia's mom agreed with the idea of helping her set up a sanctuary in her room. She helped Lydia pick out new colors for the walls that would be cheery and cozy. They put up fun art posters and created a corner with all the things Lydia wanted if she needed to feel more grounded: a fluffy blanket, a journal and supplies to write or color with, and a pillow if she needed to yell into it. Lydia and her mom agreed it would be helpful to identify when she felt chaotic inside or felt like the world around her was stressful and she would go to her space and spend time practicing grounding exercises. Lydia appreciated having her room be an area she could count on.

Rewriting Your Story

One of the frustrating things about trauma is that it isn't something you chose for yourself or dreamt for your future, and now you have to figure out how to move forward with this experience you don't want. It can create a feeling of powerlessness that leads you to dream about a way to make it like none of it ever happened. Unfortunately, healing isn't something where you just remove the bad experience. Instead, healing is finding a way to move forward with those experiences, but you are absolutely allowed to look at it differently.

Let's say you're going to do an art project. You have a whole basket of different materials that you have to use. You go through it, and most of it is fine, but you don't want to use the googly eyes. So, you say that, but you're told, "You have to use all of the materials." "Okay, but no googly eyes." "*All* of the materials." "*NO GOOGLY EYES.*" You go back and forth, fighting about the rules, but you never get a different answer. You lose time that you could be working on your project, and everyone just ends up upset. Or, you can be upset and vent your frustrations, but the sooner you get to work, the more time you have to figure out how to make it all come together. Maybe you have to use materials you don't want, like those googly eyes, but you can find a way to include them without them being the whole focus.

And that's the point: Your trauma does not have to be the focus of your life or even of your memory of what you experienced. The focus could be anything you want it to be! It can be about how you got through a hard time, how you grow from tough situations, what you learn about your own strengths and the world around you, or how you grow closer to others and figure out who your best friends are. Again, you get to decide the meaning of your experiences.

You will inevitably experience a lot of surprises in life, though hopefully, none of the others will be as negative as your traumatic experience. Regardless, you will realize that as you get older, life becomes less about how all your plans worked out perfectly and more about what you did and how you adapted when things went in a different direction. This doesn't mean you should give up goals that mean a lot to you just because there are obstacles. However, you may need to be creative and find new ways to reach those goals. Other times, teens may need to evaluate whether the goals you set in the past still suit you now. You'll get new information about yourself and what you want the more you live, and it's unrealistic to think everything will turn out exactly how you'd intended. That doesn't mean everything is ruined! It means, instead, that there are new ways you can appreciate an unexpected twist.

A traumatic experience is definitely more than just an "unexpected twist," and by definition, it changes the way you view yourself, others, and the world around you. You do not have to accept the initial meaning you or anyone else assign to this trauma. It might be difficult to make brand-new definitions of your experience when still experiencing PTSD. Instead of feeling like you have to decide on a new perspective suddenly, take your time as you work through your healing, and consider different ideas of how you want to carry your experience. You might also think of ways you would like to view the trauma in the future, acknowledging that you aren't quite there yet. Just like adapting to changing goals, your view of your story and what traumatic experiences mean to you can also change and adapt over time.

It can seem easy to fall into a world of what-ifs, focusing on how things might have been if you hadn't had your traumatic experience. Mourning what you've lost is an important task. But here's an important what-if: What if those feelings and wishes get in the way of you doing what you can with the life you have? That's another way PTSD can rob you of a happy and healthy life. No amount of anger, frustration, or sadness can change what has already happened. Building the life you want moving forward is a much more satisfying venture for your time, effort, and heart.

Many people who experience traumatic events heal from PTSD and learn something about the world *because* of their trauma that inspires them toward new goals and dreams. Through this post-traumatic growth, these people may focus on helping others who experience similar trauma. Although this is a fantastic outcome, please know that this is not required of you. You are allowed to be whoever you want to be, whether or not you make it your life's focus to help others. You are also allowed to be happy and healthy contributing to the world in a way completely unrelated to your trauma. What's important is that you heal and focus on things that matter to you.

> **"**Your view of your story . . . can also change and adapt over time.**"**

EXERCISE

Trauma disconnects us from our current experience, but expressing how we're stuck helps us move forward. This is why music, storytelling, art, and dance can be helpful outlets. Here's an expression and physical movement exercise you can do at home: Try finding a box, an upside-down pot, or maybe a stack of books. What kind of drumbeats can you make with your hands? Close your eyes and get into a rhythm that feels right for you. Are there words you can speak or sing to the beat about yourself, your trauma, or your dreams? Let your story flow.

_____

_____

_____

_____

_____

_____

_____

_____

_____

_____

_____

_____

MIDWAY CHECK-IN

How are you doing with all the information you are learning and activities you are trying? Do you have ideas for other topics you'd like to see covered here, or exercises you think would be good to include? This book is already printed, but that doesn't mean you can't add your own ideas for growth and healing. This is a chance to practice taking charge of your life and expressing your best interests. Use the box below to explain your idea.

What is the goal for your exercise? How do you do it, and how does it help?

New Exercise

Check in with yourself and see how you're feeling. Get a good stretch and take a deep breath or three. Are you only working on what you need right now, or are you maybe feeling a little burned out? It can also be tempting to try and do as much reading and as many exercises at once as you can, but this book is here to help you in the long run, so it's okay to take your time. These things usually work better when you respect where you are in the process and focus on one thing at a time. What does your body need right now? Is it water? A snack? A nap? A video of some baby cats, dogs, or lizards? All totally valid. Please listen to your body and mind and try giving them what they need right now.

Your Coping Method Tool Kit

Having multiple strategies to help you in challenging times is important. You may try out a tool, and when it doesn't completely fix the problem, decide it "doesn't work" and stop using it. Unfortunately, there is no one resource that works on its own. If, in the moment, you'd put your feeling of being overwhelmed at level 10, you probably won't find a technique that brings you right to neutral. But if you have a handful of approaches that each calm you by a few levels, you'll end up in a better place. Every tool you give yourself adds up.

But you also need to be able to define what neutral is for you. This is sometimes called the "window of tolerance." This is the emotional range where you can function well, do things you need to do, and feel okay generally—even if challenging things happen—because your emotions are regulated. Your energy fluctuates throughout the day, but so long as you manage to keep it in your window of tolerance, you do fine. Above the window, energy rises too high, leading to anxiety or anger. Below the window, energy drops too low, and you feel depressed and unmotivated. This window can be small if you've experienced something traumatic. Let's discuss ways to maintain steady energy, bring your energy down, or pull it up when needed. As you begin to understand and manage your energy and emotions, your window of tolerance grows, and handling the world becomes easier.

Maintaining within Tolerance

Although your energy fluctuates throughout the day, the goal is to keep it as stabilized and manageable as possible. Coping is a lot easier when you meet your basic needs. Keeping a regular sleep schedule will help you start the day with some sense of predictability and security. Do your best to eat when you are hungry and drink enough water. Take any prescribed medications you need. Find time to move your body each day, even just to a song you like. When your basic biological needs are met, everything else becomes a little easier to handle throughout the day.

Downregulating Energy Spikes

Sometimes your frustration levels rise through the top of your window of tolerance, and you feel anxious or angry. This focus and drive may feel productive or justified, but it comes with a high cost: It's exhausting! All your energy pours into a single issue, you crash afterward, and you may even regret things you said or did. Your body floods with cortisol, and even your cells experience stress, which can increase your chances of getting sick.

To coax yourself down when you're feeling worked up, start noticing how you feel and putting a name to it. Stating to yourself "I am feeling angry right now" helps you identify your experience while creating enough separation to decide what to do next. Inhale to the count of four and exhale to the count of six, repeating at least three times. Keep your hands open and palms up on your lap or hanging down at your sides—this also communicates to your brain that you're trying to downregulate your emotions. Try some stretches and see what feels right for your body. Meditating and labeling what you are experiencing without judgment also helps your emotional regulation. Try playing some music that helps you feel calmer and in control.

There are times when doing relaxing things doesn't help and maybe even agitates you further. If you've tried calming activities and you continue to feel on edge, try matching your energy in a healthy way instead. This can mean doing jumping jacks or putting on upbeat music that gets you going. This works because by going with the energy you convince your brain that you were only worked up because of these positive and controllable reasons. Once your brain latches on to this new "reason," it can be easier to coax it back down.

Upregulating Low Energy

When your energy drops past the bottom of your window of tolerance, you can feel depressive, sluggish, numb, and generally shut down from the world. This can happen in the aftermath of an energy spike you've experienced. This can also result from ongoing, long-term disengagement from yourself and the world around you. Finding ways to reconnect and stimulate your interests will help upregulate your energy.

When you find yourself below your window of tolerance, noticing and naming how you're feeling can lift you up, too. Tend to your biological needs, like sound sleep and nutrition, in case you've ignored any of them, either on purpose or by accident. If your needs are met, or you can't tell because you're feeling numb, try some gentle activities to start reconnection and to bring your energy up. Get a good stretch! As awkward as it might feel, fake a smile and hold it for ten seconds, or fake laughing. These are more physical tricks your brain may pick up on and go with. Find a video that makes you laugh, a song you love, or watch a movie on a topic you find interesting.

EXERCISE

Identifying your window of tolerance is a great start to managing it. How would your window look if it was a real, physical window? Draw one for yourself, on paper or digitally. How big or small is it? How would you decorate it? How does your energy flow through it during different times of day? What does it feel like to spike into the space above your window? Below it? What things happen throughout the day that push your energy in either direction? Feel free to write and draw anywhere in your window picture as you consider these questions.

Healing & Processing Your Trauma

EXERCISE

Now that you have ideas on how to lower, raise, and maintain your energy to cope through difficult times, take a moment to brainstorm more ideas for what can help you. They can be as serious or as outlandish as you want to make them. The goal, for now, is to just come up with as many ideas as possible. Once you've done this, give a number rating to how well you think the real tools will help on a scale from 1 to 10. Keep this list where you can see and use it when you need it!

MIDWAY CHECK-IN

You've gotten a look at your coping method toolbox and managing your window of tolerance, so check in with that window right now. Without changing how your body is in this moment, notice how you are feeling and where your energy is. Are you contained comfortably within your window? Are you feeling worked up right now? Has all this talk about energy pushed you below your window, leaving you disconnected and burned out? Do you hate the concept of windows and wish it was a completely different analogy? However you are feeling, take note of it.

What are some things you can do to help yourself feel more comfortable in this moment? That may look like a good stretch, some deep breaths, a snack, some hydration, or a chat with a friend. Maybe play some music, whether the songs are upbeat or slow, so long as they feel good for you right now. You've read a lot of things and hopefully learned something new. You're doing great. If you feel like you have a lot to process right now, journaling and meditating are two great ways to do that. If you'd rather get out of your head for now, trying some yoga poses or other mindful movements to the best of your ability is a great way to practice being present. Whatever you choose, be gentle with yourself.

[Tay's Story]

Tay could recount the exact moment of their trauma even though it wasn't something that happened to them directly. Something awful happened to someone across the country, and Tay saw it on the news. The images they saw were explicit, disturbing, and stuck in their mind for months to come. The person had been killed in a violent encounter, and seeing their body in videos circulating on social media made it hard to avoid. That person looked a bit like Tay, dressed like them, and could've been someone they knew if they had lived in the same area.

The news story itself had been very unlike Tay's own life, but they were completely thrown off because of it. Tay often felt on the verge of tears or like they could just scream. Other times, Tay felt like nothing mattered and had no motivation for even things they used to enjoy. Keeping up with class and work was hard when death was all Tay could think about. Their dad was upset when the next report card showed Tay was failing some classes. When he confronted them, all the frustration and despair came spilling out. How could they focus and talk about school in a time like this? Tay was surprised when their dad got quiet instead of yelling back. He shared his own distress over the event. They yelled together, cried together, and finally agreed it would be best if they both talked to a mental health professional on how to cope, heal, and find balance even in harsh times.

The Importance of a Strong Support System

Humans are social and culturally motivated creatures. We are born into relationships with family members or guardians, and we learn from our communities as we grow up. Positive connections in relationships heal us, and unhealthy disconnections in relationships bring us distress and trauma. Generally speaking, everyone benefits from experiencing external and internal acceptance, from belonging in their communities, and from the sense that they contribute in meaningful ways.

Finding and maintaining a strong support system is valuable for healing from trauma. The weight of a traumatic event is figuratively heavy, but it's easier to carry when more people are there to help. The core of a good support system is healthy relationships. Relationships help break the sense of shame PTSD can trap you in. As researcher and author Dr. Brené Brown states, "shame requires three things to grow exponentially: secrecy, silence, and judgment." If you feel like you can share your experiences with those close to you without judgment, shame cannot survive, and you will feel more empowered to heal and grow. Members of your support system can be there when you are really struggling but can also share your joys with you. If they have experience in an area you would like to know more about, you can learn from them. And they can share in even everyday life events, giving these moments new meaning.

Ideally, your family can be part of your core support system. They are often the people you are around when you're home, and home serves you best when it's a sanctuary. This may not always be possible. Sometimes family members are the people who have caused the trauma. Sometimes they are antagonistic to healing or uninterested and unhelpful. In this case, there is value in the concept of "found family" or "chosen family." These are the people with whom you share a close and positive bond that feels

> "The weight of a traumatic event is figuratively heavy, but it's easier to carry when more people are there to help."

like your idea of what family should be. Are there friends you know you can count on and who you can be there for as well? Do you have teachers, mentors, or other people you look up to? Perhaps your close friends have great parents who welcome you with open arms. Anyone you trust in this way can be a source of support and just as valid a connection as the family you are born into.

Of course, it is helpful to be cautious about who you consider your support system. This is especially true when you have gone through traumatic events and when your own family has not been supportive. There are, unfortunately, people who seem very supportive when you are going through a hard time but then turn around and somehow manipulate or take advantage of the situation. Beware of people who make it seem like you can't trust anybody but them. It might sound like they have good reasons to doubt your family and friends, but genuinely supportive people will encourage you to find as much support as possible instead of limiting your options to only them. Although friends giving mutual support can be normal and healthy, adult figures who need something from you in exchange for their support raise a potential red flag. People who make their support conditional on you doing what they want raise another red flag. Healthy and caring people want what's best for you and respect your boundaries, even if it's not in their own interests.

Once you've determined who you can count on, it's important to establish kind but open communication about needs and expectations. What kinds of things might you want to talk about together? What activities would you enjoy doing? What does it look like when you're having a hard time, and what should they do to help? What sorts of boundaries work best for you? You don't just have to talk about your traumatic experience; it's also helpful to spend time enjoying each other's company. Communication about expectations is not a one-time event—for healthy support systems, communication is ongoing and keeps everyone up to date.

You may find that some members of your support system are helpful to talk to in some situations but not others. Maybe some friends are great for when you need to get out of your head and joke around, but not great for discussing deep topics. Others might be great for helping in some life difficulties but have their own challenges with others that you'd rather not bring up. This is perfectly okay, as everyone's experience and abilities are different. Instead of hoping that everyone will be great at everything, take stock of who is best matched for which situations. This is a form of acceptance and will help keep everyone from feeling unnecessarily frustrated with each other. Some people may also need to come and go as life changes and moves forward. Kind but open communication is key. This is true, whether it's about challenges you've been through, the expectations you hold, or the ways you hope to adapt in your relationships with others.

EXERCISE

When you picture the support system you want to have, how do you expect to feel? This is a similar activity to when you thought about how you want to feel in your own sanctuary space and time. When you're around supportive people, do you think of yourself feeling calm? Encouraged? Energetic? Soft? Intelligent? Strong? Sparkly? Brainstorm some ideas of the words you'd like to feel and write or draw them out. As you interact with friends and people around you, consider whether you feel any of these descriptions. If so, this could be a sign that person or situation is one you find particularly supportive.

EXERCISE

Make some notes about the people in your support system. What do you value about each person? What do you like to talk about and do together? How do you feel when you spend time with them and share about yourself? Are there reminders you could write down, like topics they don't like talking about or can't help with? Who do you feel closest to? Who would you like to be closer to? Who feels like they may be growing away from you? It can be helpful to revisit these questions from time to time.

Name: _____

Notes: _____

_____

_____

Name: _____

Notes: _____

_____

_____

Name: _____

Notes: _____

_____

_____

CLOSING CHECK-IN

You've officially made it past the halfway point! As you wrap up this chapter, it's a good time to check in with yourself and how you're feeling in this moment. You dove into a lot of concepts, and you likely did a lot of work figuring out your own emotional regulation and the stability in your immediate environment. You learned about windows of tolerance and thought about your own. You considered the support system you have and how close it is to the system you want. Even if all you did was read a paragraph and think about the words, your neurons were busy processing that information, which takes energy. So, how are you?

Take a deep breath, hold it, and let it out in a nice, heavy sigh. Just notice what's going on in your body—feelings, thoughts, sensations. What do you need most in this moment? Tend to your biological needs first, such as food, hydration, rest, a stretch. This book will be here whenever you're ready to pick it up again. Once you've taken care of what your body needs, consider what reading this chapter was like for you. What did you like the most? Were there parts you hated? How did your trauma come up for you, if at all? Did you learn things you'd like to share with someone close to you? Feel free, as always, to highlight, make notes, and doodle whatever helps you on these pages. Journaling your thoughts on this chapter can also help you process the information. If the journaling veers off into talking about your traumatic experience, all the better. I hope you will be able to connect this information with your own experience in a helpful way. New understandings about your experience may help you find creative ways to work through it.

Now is a good time for a stretch and a nice yawn, either real or fake. This gives us the same calming effect as inhaling longer than we exhale and sighing out a deep breath: the breathing pattern signals to the brain that we are safe and that we can be calm. Nobody sighs, after all, while they are still running from a tiger. Sighing comes after! Take note of what time it is, what day it is, and what season it is. What did you do earlier in the day, before you sat down with this book? What do you have to do next today? Taking time to remember these things is helpful for grounding, because it reminds us of where and when we are. The more you connect to yourself and your present, the more unstuck you become from your PTSD.

Key Takeaways

Welcome to the end of chapter 3. Hopefully, you have begun building a sense of safety for yourself and have practiced managing your emotions and energy during challenging moments. You may already notice a shift in your experience as you practice. Let's review the big takeaways for this chapter:

* PTSD is destabilizing. Establishing safety and stability is an important starting point before unraveling traumatic experiences. Without this, trying to process trauma can become complicated and even re-traumatizing. One way to build safety and stability is by building a specific place for yourself dedicated to that purpose. Sometimes space is limited and can't be changed. It's perfectly acceptable to make a portable "sanctuary" you can take with you using grounding items (see page 57). You can also choose times to spend in your safe space and dedicate these times to recharging and processing.

* PTSD overrides the way your brain is used to storing memories and telling your stories. However, your story is yours! You get to determine the meaning of your experiences. How might this be a story of strength, hope, and connection? Although you can't simply cut out the trauma, you can choose how you see it as time goes on. Mourn what you may have lost but focus on what you want to do next.

* One tool is not enough to combat strong emotions, much less the challenges of PTSD. Your energy can fluctuate throughout the day and pull you in and out of emotional regulation or your windows of tolerance. Tending to basic biological needs can help you maintain a steady emotional baseline. Many tools can help you downregulate an emotional spike or upregulate an energy slump. Figuring out which ones work best for you in advance will help you know what to do when you need them.

- Healing and everyday living both work best in healthy connections with others. Immediate family is a great place to start but may not be a guarantee for everyone. Thankfully, you can also connect with friends, teachers, and others you can count on or look up to. Not everyone deserves your trust, so it's important to identify the ones who honor your boundaries. People may come and go, but respectful communication and acceptance of everyone's differences are what sustain a strong support system.

This chapter focused on building your internal strength through stability and techniques for managing your emotional experience. The peace you build inside will help you as you interact with others around you. The next chapter will focus on exactly that: the challenges of PTSD when you need to engage with others. It's not easy work, but it is worthwhile. You are most worthwhile.

CHAPTER 4

Managing PTSD in a Fast-Paced World

The previous chapters have covered the basics of what to do and how to do it in terms of healing your PTSD. Steps like tending to your needs and symptoms while building your self-management skills will take you far. In this chapter, you'll discover how to troubleshoot when internal or external obstacles make those steps difficult. Nobody would need these troubleshooting tools in ideal conditions, but real life can bring unexpected challenges. You may have difficulty recognizing your needs in the moment. You may face challenges voicing those needs to others. Boundaries may feel impossible to make or keep. Perhaps your current relationships are more harmful to you than helpful. This isn't a direct reflection of you; this reflects how complicated being human is. Although you can't predict every personal obstacle, there are many you can prepare for. With some practice and adjustments as you go along, these will be areas you can grow in. These skills will benefit both your PTSD healing and your effective communication in general.

This chapter will first explore some of the potential internal challenges, starting with understanding what you need for yourself. If you don't know how to advocate for yourself, and others don't understand how to help you, the result is a lot of frustration and further difficulty. You'll learn how to figure out what you need and how to ask for it, which greatly increases the chance you will have that need fulfilled. Then you'll explore how to be comfortable speaking your truth and authenticity even though you've experienced difficulties and trauma. This will include creative ways to express your feelings and be honest through challenging parts of your story. You'll learn how to set up and maintain boundaries for yourself so you can stay safe and honor your needs. As you do, you'll identify the most vital person for holding your boundaries and respecting your needs: you. Finally, you'll discover ways to identify and cut out toxicity to protect your healing and growth. This will include discussing how to appreciate what you have learned from both helpful and challenging relationships while giving them space to end if needed.

Here's a checklist of these topics so you can look ahead at the chapter, keep track of what you've read, and make notations about anything you might want to review or remember. You're free to read these in any order that works for you and revisit any topics at any time. This is your book to mark up, highlight, and doodle through.

☐ How to Ask for What You Need

☐ Getting Comfortable Speaking Your Truth

☐ Creating & Maintaining Boundaries

☐ Cutting Out Toxicity

[Nick's Story]

Nick was frustrated with the people in his support system. They had all seemed fine before, but he found them increasingly inconsiderate after his traumatic experience and PTSD diagnosis. Sometimes their normal conversations would bother him, whether it was the topic or how loud they spoke, and they wouldn't notice. There were times he wanted their company and times he wanted to be alone, but they never seemed to get it right. Nick would even make angry exits when he'd had enough, but they'd just act confused and oblivious to what they had done. It felt like the people who should be there for him didn't care at all about his needs and wants.

Nick brought up his frustration and hurt to his therapist. Here were friends and family, but what good were they if they weren't supporting him in his healing? Nick's therapist listened closely and validated how frustrated and disappointed he felt. Then she asked, "What happens when you talk to them about how you're feeling?" Nick shrugged. "I don't," he said. "I don't want to talk to them when I feel like this." Nick's therapist then gently asked whether he might be hoping his support system knew what he needed without his asking, or if he was explicitly asking for what he needed and giving them the opportunity to decide either way. Nick was quiet for a long moment. He hadn't realized he'd been expecting his support system to read his mind. Nick decided it was time to start expressing his needs.

How to Ask for What You Need

Asking those around you for what you need is important. You might feel as if those who care about you *should* be able to understand what you need and when. Unfortunately, caring about others doesn't grant anyone mind-reading powers or the ability to interpret subtle signals. Although you may have some friends and family who seem to understand without being told, they are not guaranteed to get it right every time without your input. The best way to increase your chances of getting what you need is to ask!

The first question to ask is for yourself: What, in fact, do you need? The answer can be unclear if you feel mixed up, frustrated, or stressed out. The human brain isn't the best at problem-solving and logical processing during strong emotional experiences. The more you practice noticing and labeling how you feel and what you think, the easier it will become. However, there will still be times when your needs are not straightforward and you're not sure how to interpret them in the moment. In those cases, it can help to have a few go-to questions and solutions prepared. Try out the following for a start:

Do you feel apathetic or numb to everything and everyone? Do you not care right now about past, present, or future? When asking yourself what you want, is your answer to everything "no," including whether you still like your goals, want to change them, or want to give up completely? ➜ When nothing means anything to you, and you do not want absolutely anything, chances are you are pretty burnt out and really tired. Try and get some good, deep sleep before reconsidering your activities and life goals. Once you're better rested, consider whether you have taken on too many tasks and if you can let go of some.

Do you feel generally irritable? Are everyone and everything getting on your nerves? ➜ If you feel like you hate everything right now, that's usually a strong sign you have basic needs you need to take care of. This includes eating and getting some regular physical activity to the best of your abilities. If you experience this irritability regularly and over a long period of time, this can also be a sign you are prioritizing other people over your own needs.

Now that you have identified what you need in this moment, continue practicing this regularly. Check in with yourself throughout the day by asking yourself, "What do I need right now?" Do your best to follow through with the solutions you can handle yourself.

So, how do you feel about asking others for what you need? Do you worry about bothering them? Many people are happy to help. If they don't want to, they are allowed to say no. Simply asking in a kind and honest way isn't rude. The goal is to be assertive in your request. Not like this: "Your show is so loud. Quit being inconsiderate and turn it down." This aggressive approach will probably increase conflict between the two of you, and they'll be less interested in helping you. And then there's the passive approach. This would be not to say anything and hope they turn down the television anyway. A passive-aggressive approach might be to sigh loudly and say, "Wow, the television is loud." This might communicate a fact, but it's not a direct request, and it requires others to guess what you want. Is it just a statement that doesn't need action? Are you asking them to do something? They may turn down the television but may also resent that they had to work to figure out what you want. An assertive request is straightforward, does not cast judgments, and simply asks for what you'd like: "Can you turn down the television, please? A little bit is fine."

There may be times when others aren't willing or able to grant your requests. They may ask for clarification or more details. Whether you choose to give these depends on you and your relationship with this other person. You get to decide what you share and when. If someone is willing and able to grant your request, great! If they're not, it's then up to you to take care of your needs, even if the solution isn't what you originally hoped for. Perhaps you wanted the volume turned down so you could focus on journaling, but you have a family member who has hearing loss. Alternative options may be finding earplugs or moving to a different room to do your activity. You can ask for others to help you but following through on what you need is ultimately your responsibility.

"You get to decide what you share and when."

EXERCISE

Sometimes it's hard to identify and prioritize what you need, especially if you are used to putting other people first. For this exercise, think about the part of you that is the quickest to feel angry or mean. This part of you is often the place that holds the most hurt. This part of you is doing its best to handle everything, even if it isn't kind about it. How does this part of you feel right now? Is it okay or upset? If you were going to try and kindly help it, what would it need? This is a great starting point to understanding how you feel and coming up with ideas for meeting your needs.

_____

_____

_____

_____

_____

_____

_____

_____

_____

_____

_____

_____

_____

MIDWAY CHECK-IN

Take a few moments and check in with yourself. Get a good stretch, inhale, and sigh it out. What do you think about what you've learned today? How has your day been going? Has reading and doing these activities been clear, or have you been distracted by something else? Sometimes events throughout the day catch our attention, and until we give ourselves time to think through them, they stick in the back of our minds and pop up when we're trying to focus. You might also find that you've been able to focus well, but all the new information feels like it's swirling around in your head without taking a clear shape.

Grab paper and pen, a note-taking app, or a voice-recording app—whatever is accessible to you—and do a brain dump. Write, type, or speak out all the pieces of things on your mind right now. It doesn't matter if they are related or not, and they don't even need to be complete sentences or more than a word or two each. Let everything spill out without judgment. Once you've written or said everything on your mind, take a moment to just breathe in the space left over. How are you? What would serve you best right now? Consider how to take care of yourself in this moment.

[Sakura's Story]

After some initial work on connecting and trusting her therapist, Sakura began feeling comfortable talking about herself and her traumatic experience. She had taken steps to make her everyday life feel safe and stable. She was doing her best to maintain a sense of routine in her life. The next focus for healing from PTSD, her therapist said, was to find ways to express the trauma she had experienced. Sakura had already felt some relief from simply talking about the trauma event instead of holding it in secrecy, but there were still feelings and ideas she wasn't sure how to put into words. There were vague feelings and pieces of memories. She wanted to express them and get them out, but she wasn't sure how.

Sakura's therapist introduced her to art therapy after learning that she had always enjoyed creative activities and crafts. Sakura started with tearing pictures out of magazines and making a collage to represent her current state of mind. As she neared the end of the collage project, she felt like painting over the collage would help express her feelings more accurately. Her artistic choices helped her therapist understand how she felt, but they also helped Sakura's understanding. She continued to personalize her projects, work with her hands, and share with those close to her the meanings of what she had created. Although it was hard to put some thoughts into words, she found describing them through colors, shapes, and textures made communicating her experience easier. For Sakura, a visual representation she'd made herself was an empowering way to share her story.

Getting Comfortable
Speaking Your Truth

It's not uncommon to want to ignore a traumatic event, to imagine that if you simply never think or talk about it, you'll be able to move on with the life you had before. Unfortunately, traumatic events upset the way people think about themselves and the world. Trying to ignore that impact holds you more tightly where you are. Your brain will try to process the fact that something world-changing has happened, yet, because you're actively suppressing thoughts about the event, you're not allowing the brain to process it fully. The result is even more stress, pressure, confusion, and flashbacks. Speaking your truths is essential for your mind, body, and soul.

By finding ways to express your experiences and feelings deliberately, you engage the prefrontal cortex, allowing your brain to identify, sort through, and store what you've been through in an adaptive way. Research shows that when a person can name their experiences, the left hemisphere of their brain releases calming neurotransmitters to the right hemisphere of their brain. We immediately begin to feel less distress because our experience has been recognized. Expressing ourselves and having others understand us is extremely satisfying on many levels!

So how should you express your experiences? Simply having the conversation and talking about what happened with someone you consider safe and validating is a great option. However, there is a difference between intentionally choosing to share about yourself and feeling like those experiences come tumbling out of you unintentionally. That second kind of sharing feels pressured; it is a bit uncontrollable and is more common earlier in the healing process. With time, effort, and patience, the goal is to stop sharing by accident and start doing it on purpose so you feel like you're directing your own experience. Therapeutic practice, either with a mental health professional or self-guided activities, will help get that energy under control and allow you to choose what you want to say and how.

> "When a person can name their experiences, the left hemisphere of their brain releases calming neurotransmitters."

One of the great things about artistic expression is that you can use it even when your trauma experiences feel like they might take over. A sense of safety and control can come from letting an experience loose in a journal, an art piece, or movement. Being very angry can be helpful when working with clay, for example, because it takes a lot of hand strength you can direct your strong emotions into. Dance, even free-form by yourself, helps release energy stuck in your body.

Sometimes, a part of our stories casts us or people we care about in an unfavorable light. You may regret your choices or how you responded to a tough situation. You may have been careless about the effects of your behavior on others. In your struggle with your trauma, you may have even inflicted trauma on others. These can be difficult realities to accept. How do you express something that challenges how you see yourself and the people around you?

The first goal in this kind of difficult communication is to let yourself really look at the choices you have made in the past. Try to see these actions with honesty, not judgment. In these moments, you can remind yourself not to get caught up in deciding what makes a person "good" or "bad," because this doesn't always leave room for people to be complicated (which we all are!). Instead, you can look at it this way: We are all people, and we all make good and bad decisions. We can accept our complications while working to be better in the future. This is where acceptance and forgiveness come into play. Acceptance is not the same as approval. You can accept something has happened without saying you like it. That's true for actions, too. You are better off accepting what you have done and the consequences while doing your best to improve moving forward. You might have made mistakes in the past, but you get to decide to learn, grow, and do better. Over time and with your efforts to heal and grow, the choices you've made in the past will be a tiny detail compared to the full picture of the person you've decided to become.

Integrity is another piece of the healing puzzle. Integrity means being honest about yourself when you share your stories. Some people will respect your honesty and how you have chosen to learn from your mistakes and complicated decisions. Other people might be biased against those details and

66Acceptance is not the same as approval.99

not respect the growth you have chosen for yourself. You may unexpectedly gain or lose friendships. Accepting this possibility and the decisions of others is part of accountability. It's difficult to lose people because of how they see you, but maintaining a pleasant but dishonest image of yourself for others is unfair both to others and to you. Lying about yourself only increases the pressure you feel as you try to juggle the stories you've told. Instead, honesty gives you the freedom to just be yourself. Vulnerability and honesty may be uncomfortable, but they allow you to heal and grow.

EXERCISE

When you're ready, take some time to think through your story. How do you want to talk about the different parts of your experience? You may find that some parts of the story feel like a green light, yellow light, or red light when it comes to how easy it is to talk about. Where do you find yourself pausing? Do you worry about how some parts make you or others sound? Breathe into any discomfort you feel as you practice the harder parts. Getting comfortable with honesty about the hard parts will bring you the freedom to keep growing in life.

_____

_____

_____

_____

_____

_____

_____

_____

_____

_____

_____

_____

_____

_____

MIDWAY CHECK-IN

We live in a world with many gray areas rather than clear black and white. We might still care about those who have harmed us. We might struggle to accept ourselves after we've harmed others. Having a positive impact on the world doesn't necessarily mean always making the best choices. It often means taking responsibility for the outcomes of decisions and choosing to keep learning, growing, and improving.

Have you thought of some creative ways you'd like to express your own unique, complex thoughts and emotions? If you find yourself worrying that you're "not creative enough" to do artistic activities, remember that the ways you choose to express yourself don't have to be for anyone else; they are for you to help you process your experience. Whether you share what you make with anyone else is entirely your choice. You may also find the act of making art is the most helpful for you and that the outcome is less important.

Get a good stretch and a nice, deep breath. Look around you. How was your day? How are you feeling, and what would best serve you right now? A break and a pleasant activity might be in order. Find a way to enjoy a few minutes of today.

Creating & Maintaining Boundaries

Sometimes people dislike the idea of a boundary, because it sounds like a limitation. Feeling upset when you are told what to do, even if you wanted to do that exact thing in the first place, is called "reactance." It's a way to try to maintain a sense of independence. Boundaries, however, don't have to interfere with your free choice. Boundaries are simply recognizing what you need to be safe, happy, and healthy. You can be accountable to yourself by making and respecting your own boundaries instead of pushing against those set by others. When you protect your needs, you are holding those boundaries.

For example, say you decide you need to be in bed with the lights off by 11:30 p.m. to feel rested in the morning. You tell yourself that's what you need, and you decide to make a boundary to protect this need. So, you decide to make an evening routine and figure out that you need to start it at, say, 10:30 p.m. Then you decide to communicate this to your family: "I want to be in bed and ready to sleep by 11:30 at night, so I need to start getting ready for bed at 10:30." You're letting them know it will help you if they respect this and do not try, for example, to get you to watch a movie while you are getting ready for bed. Hopefully, they will be supportive.

However, if they forget or choose to ignore your boundary, it's your job to maintain your boundary and honor your routine. They can decide they want to watch a movie at 10:30 by themselves, but respecting your boundary means you go ahead and get ready for bed anyway. Maybe they pressure you to stay up just this one time but are usually happy to support your needs. Or perhaps they are constantly making fun of your decisions and disrespecting your needs and boundaries. If this is the case, you may try to have a serious, honest, and hopeful conversation with them. You may explain how their treatment of your decisions has made you feel, as well as how you hope they can be more supportive in the future.

There are times when they choose to ignore you or respond with anger despite your best efforts to communicate with those around you. This is often a reflection of the difficulties they themselves are experiencing. Some people have trouble accepting accountability and working toward growth without feeling overwhelming shame. It's not your job, however, to comfort someone who is upset because you told them something they did upset you. This is a discomfort they need to come to terms with. Other people don't have to share your goals, interests, or boundaries, but it is important they respect you enough to value what you find important. If you approach others kindly but firmly about your needs, and they cannot or will not be supportive, the next decision about your boundaries is yours to make. The main person who needs to support your boundaries is you.

In another example, you may have a boundary for yourself around not drinking alcohol and not being in places where you'll be tempted to drink. You might communicate that decision to your friends and ask them not to drink around you or to let you know if drinking will happen at a get-together so you can avoid it. But then you show up at a party, and people are drinking, but your friends didn't warn you. You find them and ask them about it, and they just shrug. However you might feel toward your friends for not warning you, the next decision is yours: Do you stay, or do you respect the boundary you set and leave? Sure, you might be disappointed in missing out and annoyed that you're leaving on your own, but you are prioritizing your needs and taking your boundaries seriously.

Boundaries are not punishments for yourself or others. Boundaries are for protecting what you need to survive and thrive. Sometimes, though, you may be hurt and scared and create boundaries that keep people out completely. You might even distance yourself from people who can help you because you feel too vulnerable to the world. By giving yourself gentle space to heal and spending time around kind and patient people, you can learn to create boundaries that help instead of getting in the way.

Imagine you have a nice garden. Think of this as the garden of your life, in which you plant all that is pleasing to you. Without any boundaries, everyone can come in and take all the plants and flowers and step all over the things you've spent so much time carefully planting. What a disaster! So, you build a very tall wall that nobody can see into or climb over. You stay inside the wall alone and tend to your garden. You might have a very nice garden again, but now you can't share it with anyone. Plus, the wall might keep out some of the light and air needed for your garden to grow how you'd like. Healthy boundaries, instead, are like a fence with a gate around your garden. People can come and look if you'd like, but you get to determine who comes in, what they are allowed to do, and how long they stay.

"Boundaries are not punishments for yourself or others."

EXERCISE

Take a moment and consider what decisions and protections you can make for your health and well-being. What are some changes you'd like to make at home? School? Work? With other people? These ideas are potential boundaries you can choose to support for yourself. For example, you might have a habit of saying "yes" to too many requests because you like to help others. But then you end up overwhelmed. So, you can create a boundary like "I will not take on any new projects for the next month" or "I will say 'Let me think about it' then get back to them." What are some statements like this that you could make for yourself?

_____

_____

_____

_____

_____

_____

_____

_____

_____

_____

_____

EXERCISE

Consider the members of your support system, as well as people outside it, and journal your observations. Who respects you when you say no or otherwise express a boundary? Who has trouble with it? Are you interested in having conversations with them and giving them a chance to be more supportive? Are there people you have provided with too many opportunities at the cost of what's good for you? What makes it difficult to support your boundaries around them? Remember that boundaries are simply protections for what you need to be healthy and happy. You deserve them.

_____

_____

_____

_____

_____

_____

_____

_____

_____

_____

_____

_____

MIDWAY CHECK-IN

What do you think about all this boundary talk? Has your perspective changed on boundaries? How would you describe boundaries you've put up in the past: a tall, inaccessible wall, a firm but adaptable fence and gate, or perhaps nothing at all? What would you like your boundaries to look like in the future? You might feel open about some parts of your life and protective about others. It's perfectly fine to recognize these differences and serve each need individually. Consider writing about or drawing a representation of these different boundaries and what goes inside each.

Take a nice, deep breath in, hold it, then let it out. Look around the space you are in. What do you see around you? What time of day is it? How long have you been reading today? How has your week been so far? Take this time to check in with yourself and how you are feeling. It might be time for a drink of water, some movement and stretching, or a different activity. Talking about boundaries may touch on tender and vulnerable parts of yourself. If you feel that right now, maybe a spot in your chest or stomach, take a moment to inhale deeply and imagine the air going right to that space. This visualization will help you relax around those places, and that relaxation promotes healing.

[*Chantelle's Story*]

Chantelle always did as she was told to avoid being in trouble—this was her response to trauma. However, as she began to heal, she learned more about her own boundaries and values. She started to consider what kind of person she wanted to be and how to stand up for what she believed in. Chantelle didn't expect to practice this with her boss, but one day they asked her to make false claims to customers to increase sales. Chantelle felt uncomfortable lying. She felt scared when she found out these types of lies were illegal. After thinking it over, Chantelle came up with a new suggestion to help sales while also being honest. She let her boss know she was not comfortable lying, then presented her new idea to help the company.

Chantelle's boss brushed off her concerns and reiterated their request that Chantelle lie. Although this job was important to Chantelle, she decided that avoiding illegal actions was more important to who she was as a person. She realized she could lose her job and would have a hard time finding a new one. Chantelle maintained her anti-lying stance while continuing to offer her new and ethical idea at work. Her boss became very unhappy with her, expecting Chantelle to do what she was told. They did not immediately fire her, but Chantelle knew that looking for a new job was a wise next step. Even so, she felt peace and empowerment for having maintained her boundary.

Cutting Out Toxicity

There are times when you might have to decide whether staying connected with someone is causing you harm. You might have told someone many times that you don't appreciate certain treatment or behavior. Maybe they said they would support your boundary but keep disrespecting it. Maybe they have been hostile or mocking about your needs from the start. There might not have been any pattern at all, just an unexpected act of disregard for your boundaries. It's up to you to figure out whether your connection to someone is more helpful or painful. This can be particularly difficult if that person is part of your family, a longtime close friend, or someone you are romantically connected to. Unfortunately, toxic dynamics can be present in any relationship.

Maintaining healthy relationships and letting go of harmful ones is a vital part of the healing process and a satisfying life. The first stage to recovering from trauma, as we've explored, is establishing safety within yourself and the world around you. If someone in your life is constantly putting you down or disregarding your needs, this is not a safe environment to heal and grow in. Instead, your brain registers that negativity as a stressful attack. Your brain is primed for safety first and will use all the available mental and emotional resources to prioritize coping and surviving through that current, toxic relationship instead of healing from and processing PTSD. So, although it is not always easy or pleasant in the moment, getting rid of unhealthy connections is important for your healing.

Is there a person who comes to mind on the subject of disrespecting you and your boundaries? How would you describe your emotions when you're around that person? How do you feel about yourself when you're with them? Do you feel like you can trust them? Does their input and influence in your life lead you toward healing or away from it? Do you feel you can grow and expand with this person, or do you feel yourself shrink around them? The people and experiences that help us expand, grow, and heal are generally the ones we want to keep around.

Accountability in setting and maintaining boundaries means recognizing that ending a connection is your decision. The other person is free to think or respond however they'd like—that part is not your responsibility.

> **"Your well-being is more important than what others think about you."**

Ideally, you'll be able to express your decision and any appropriate reasons. Looking back at the example where you were invited to a party without being told about alcohol there, you might say, "I want to protect my decision not to be around alcohol anymore. You haven't been as supportive about that boundary as I need, so I'm going to spend time with other friends from now on." If protecting your needs around this person or situation is overly complicated, however, you don't have to make a statement. You can choose to block, ghost, unfollow, or otherwise stop engaging as it works for you. They may feel hurt or confused or have all kinds of opinions about how you chose to cut ties but accepting that possibility is part of your decision. It's a big one, but it's yours to make. Your well-being is more important than what others think about you.

You do not have to convince someone you are cutting ties with to agree with you. They may tell you it doesn't make sense or ask "why" many times and in different ways. You don't have to give them every single "reason" they ask for. They may be stalling the end of the relationship and expressing their unhappiness without accepting accountability. By pressuring you to justify your choice, they continue to make you responsible for the problem. This is like blaming you overall. Whatever their reaction, your boundaries could look like sticking to what you've already told them and then ending the conversation. They might accept the change, or they might be angry. They might feel something in between. Regardless, you have the right to make your decision and stick to it. They are going to believe whatever they decide to believe about you. Other people's opinions are not something you can control. Focus on what you need for your well-being. It might be painful in the moment, but your happiness is totally worth it.

What about people you will always be connected to? Sometimes it's a family member who is behaving in a toxic manner. You may always be related to that person, but you don't have to engage with them, spend time with them, or talk to them if it prevents you from healing. Your decisions are valid and belong to you. It doesn't matter what someone else, even another family member, thinks they would have done, or what they would be willing to put up with in their own life. Your limits belong to you and are worth your respect, even if others don't agree. You may live with toxic relationships in a household you cannot leave. You may be dependent on a job where you are being mistreated. If something like this is the case, do your best to protect yourself and your needs while making healthy outside connections and working toward a way out. Your immediate safety is the most important thing.

EXERCISE

It's hard to stand up for what we need sometimes, but so much easier to support the people around us. Pretend for a moment that you are looking at yourself as a different person—like your best friend. There are all the same worries, concerns, and difficulties; only they belong to this best-friend version of you now. What would you say to them? How would you encourage them? What do they need to know about themselves? Write these things down where you can see and revisit them easily.

_____

_____

_____

_____

_____

_____

_____

_____

_____

_____

_____

_____

_____

_____

CLOSING CHECK-IN

It's time to check in with yourself and what you've read in this chapter. What stood out to you? What was new or strange? What did you already know? Most important, how do you think this information will work with your experience? Have you thought about boundaries you'd like to set or remove in your connection to others? Since we talked about artistic expression, consider taking a moment to make up a haiku about how this information applies to you. Use five syllables for the first line, seven for the second, and five for the last. Expressing yourself with predetermined rules is one way to flex your creativity while processing your experience enough to fit those rules. And it's a good way to test out a low-stakes boundary. Here's an example:

Am I too open?

Am I getting what I need?

I should support me.

_____

_____

_____

When you're done, mentally scan your body to see if you feel any tension or pain. Where do you tend to carry your stress? In your neck or shoulders? Perhaps in your stomach or your legs. Wherever you find it, see what it feels like to take a deep breath and imagine the air going right into that space. This is a good signal to your brain that you'd like those muscles to release some of that tension gently.

How are you feeling in this moment? Which needs are asking for immediate attention? It can be easy to forget or ignore everyday things like eating, sleeping, staying hydrated, using the restroom, and getting regular movement. But these things will allow you to feel better more often and more consistently. Take the opportunity to put this book down and take care of yourself. You've done a really great job learning about some difficult topics. Advocating for yourself and speaking up for yourself, especially when it's uncomfortable, is a hard concept to master, with or without traumatic experience.

Keep in mind, as well, that not everything you do has to be serious, focused, and 100 percent about hard work and growth all the time. You don't need to dedicate every moment of the rest of your life to trying to follow all these new suggestions. Any change requires a lot of energy and being hard on yourself about this process will only exhaust you. Take time to rest and do fun things unrelated to any of this work. That's important for your health, too. You are allowed to take your time, do what you can, and let yourself live in the meantime. Small, deliberate changes will add up.

Key Takeaways

Great work—you've reached the end of chapter 4. You have covered some challenging aspects of healing and explored communication internally with yourself, as well as externally with others. Hopefully, you feel more acquainted with yourself and the things you need. You may also feel more ready to begin advocating for yourself to others. Let's review the main points for this chapter:

- People can't read your mind. Those very close to you may understand some of what you need before you tell them, and you can increase that understanding by voicing your thoughts and needs. Rather than feel frustrated when the people around you don't "get it," you can give them a chance by telling them what you'd like.

- Voicing needs is harder when you don't actually realize your needs. Spend time with yourself and meditate on your thoughts, feelings, and wants. This means noticing and experiencing discomfort and pain when it arises. The sooner you identify discomfort, the sooner you can adjust it and improve your experience.

- Expressing yourself brings neurological relief and allows you to be more in control of your story, as well as how you tell it. Artistic expression, such as writing, painting, and movement, provides the opportunity to process your experience while creating something cool in the process.

- Telling difficult parts of your story, including parts where you or others made unhealthy decisions, is part of processing trauma. When you are accountable for yourself and strive to do better, you open the door to healing, both for yourself and for others who were affected.

- Your boundaries protect your needs and respect what will keep you happy and healthy. Although voicing a boundary can feel uncomfortable at first, supportive people will respect your needs and do their best to help. If they cannot, you're then responsible for taking measures to keep yourself safe.

- If your relationship with someone is getting in the way of your health and growth, consider ending that connection if possible. That other person might not be happy and may even become hostile about your decision, but it's better not to be connected to toxic situations. Unhealthy relationships, including those with family members, can keep you stuck and unable to heal.

You now have many of the tools you will likely need for your healing and the challenges you may face with yourself and others. Review this information as much as you need. The more you practice and get used to understanding yourself and advocating for yourself to others, the easier it will get. In the next chapter, we will talk about the future and what you might expect as you move forward.

CHAPTER 5

Your Future Is Bright

Welcome to the last chapter of this book! In the past chapters, you've looked at what PTSD is, how it forms, and how its effects can be particularly challenging for teens. You now know the importance of building safety and stability inside and out, as well as putting together and maintaining a strong support system. You've learned some tools for managing emotions and thoughts as they pop up and how to identify your needs and advocate for them in your relationships. Now that you know how to handle the past and present, it's time to look forward to the future. You can't change what has happened in the past, but you have a multitude of futures ahead of you to pick from and build toward.

The goal for this chapter is to help you feel prepared and encouraged to continue building the life you want to live, regardless of what you have been through. As you have learned, life is unpredictable, but that doesn't have to be a negative. You will have good days, bad days, and all sorts of days in between. This chapter will discuss how healing is a process and may look different from person to person. It'll explain what to do when you encounter a setback. Struggling with an obstacle doesn't mean you have failed! Setbacks and the way you continue forward are both normal parts of the healing process. You'll circle back to the boundaries you have set for yourself so you can reevaluate them and change what they look like for you as needed. Finally, you'll discover the way your healing work fights the cycles of trauma in the world around you. After all, you are part of many systems in the world, both small and large. The healthy changes and growth you make will impact each of those systems, creating small improvements for everyone you encounter.

Here's a checklist of the main topics for this chapter. Look ahead and skip around if you'd like. Keep track of the ones you've read and the ones you would like to return to. Take your time working through the following pages. Read them in order, out of order, or upside down if that's what serves you best. Make notes, mark up the pages, and draw in the margins if it helps you process better. What is most important is that you know your options are endless, and this book is here to support you in your infinite capacity.

- ☐ Healing Isn't Linear
- ☐ Surviving Setbacks
- ☐ How to Reevaluate or Redefine Boundaries
- ☐ How You Can Help End the Trauma Cycle

[*Jess's Story*]

Jess has good days and bad days. Before they started treatment for PTSD, it seemed like all they had were bad days. Then, as they built safety and worked on their symptoms, they began to feel moments of relief. Before long, those moments would stretch longer and give them a few days of hope at a time. Their emotional overflows and intrusive thoughts quieted. But the thought of slipping back into bad days seemed scary. As Jess continued practicing their skills, however, the life they wanted to live slowly took form.

Suddenly, one night, an awful nightmare took Jess by surprise. What they saw upset them deeply. They tried to forget about it. They felt agitated and compulsively avoided old triggers all day. Jess sat on the couch that night, upset and exhausted. Why were all these old behaviors and fears popping back up? It had been years since they felt this bad. It was then Jess remembered the show they had watched the night before. Although there had been no explicit trauma, there had been a hint of something like Jess's trauma experience. They had thought little of the situation at the time, but clearly, it triggered the nightmare. Following what they had learned when first healing, Jess told their best friend about both the show and the nightmare instead of keeping it locked inside. As they cried about what they had seen and the connection to their trauma, they felt the pressure drain away. Jess was going to be fine. This was just one hard day in a sea of good days.

Healing Isn't Linear

Life gets messy. And it's a marvel that humans can grow within such an unpredictable space. Each of us are amazing organisms who started as rapidly dividing cells, and now we have lives, memories, and hopes. The fact that we, as a species, can communicate and agree on meanings for ideas is pretty incredible. We are each so different, and so is our life experience. As such, every person takes a unique path on their road to healing, and that healing is fluid rather than linear. That is, healing doesn't take a straight, sequential, time-sensitive path—it finds its own way in its own time through your unique experience.

It would be convenient if healing was, in fact, linear. You could predict your exact path and set dates for when you would reach certain and permanent milestones in your growth. You would know exactly what you would experience and when. There would never be any surprises or unexpected events. But, if that were the case, humans would have so much guaranteed predictive power, traumatic experiences would be possible to avoid from the outset.

In some way, you are different than every other person who exists, has existed, or will exist. Even if you had clones of yourself, all with your same memories and abilities, their experiences would diverge from you and each other as you all made your way through life. Even if you all did the same things, where you stood next to each other in that space would give you all slightly different perspectives. You have special connections and relationships with each person you know, which are likely different from their relationships and connections with other people. So, with your individual perspective and way of understanding the world, your trauma affects you in unique ways, and your healing will come in a unique way as well.

This isn't to say you can't map a general idea of what to expect. This just means you can get an idea and then understand it will be flexible. According to psychiatrist and researcher Dr. Judith Herman (and as you've learned), it's important to establish a sense of safety in the present, to move forward into the second stage of remembrance and mourning for what has happened and what you have lost. However, her three stages of healing are considered fluid and not bound by time. This means you might spend some time establishing safety for yourself, dip into remembrance and mourning, then go back into establishing safety for a while. You might start considering the third stage—integrating your experience and creating beautiful new connections with yourself and the world—then find yourself having to focus on safety or mourning again. This is normal and to be expected. Once you have satisfied your needs in one stage; you might even decide that you'd like to stay there for now and not worry about the next stage. That's okay, too. You can't always predict what you will need in the next day or even the next moment. Rather than pushing yourself to conform to expectations, you are better off caring for your active needs.

So, how are you supposed to figure out your healing when things change and are unique and unpredictable? The answer is in many of the exercises and check-ins we've done throughout this book: You check in with yourself, figure out what you need in that moment, and honor that need in the direction of your goals. You find ways to understand new information in ways that work for your preferred means of expression, and you continue to learn and grow as a person. Dr. Siegel describes these challenges in life as a river flowing between opposite banks of rigidity and chaos. We can get stuck against either extreme or bounce between. The goal is to strike a good balance of ourselves in the middle, where we have structure with flexibility. We can adapt to and integrate our experiences in a healthy way.

It's unlikely to strike that balance once and be perfectly settled for the rest of your life. Maintaining balance takes constant adjustments and work. You will find yourself returning to thoughts, memories, feelings, and processes you had previously mastered because you now have a different perspective or concern. The things you continue practicing are things you will continue to grow in. Conversely, your skill in areas you do not practice will decrease over time.

The upside to this constant change is that, by simply living the kind of life you want, you will make it easier to live that life in the future as well. When you focus on honoring your needs and personal values, you will be the kind of person who does so easily. When you practice your ability to

“By simply living the kind of life you want, you will make it easier to live that life in the future as well.”

express yourself appropriately and calm your nerves when you feel rattled, you make it easier to do this in the future, too. It's easy to look at the world around you and feel frustrated or even hopeless about the difficulties and challenges you see and experience. The fact that you will continue to grow stronger and more capable, even while you deal with the effects of your traumatic experience, is a wonderful and amazing testament to human life and adaptability. Life doesn't necessarily get easier; you just get stronger and better at it.

EXERCISE

Healing, as you explored, is not linear but follows a much less predictable path. What has your healing looked like since your traumatic experience? Consider drawing or graphing it for a week. Are there many ups and downs? Does it look like scribbles or loops in some areas? After a week, look at your drawing or graph. Where are the ups and downs? If you rated the lowest low and highest high, what does your range of experience look like this week? Good and bad times come and go, and you have continued forward through them all.

EXERCISE

Now that you've drawn or graphed your experience, describe what you've learned about yourself throughout this book using just key words. What values are important to you? What are the words that describe how you want to feel? Take some time to jot down or doodle these words and ideas. Maybe you value "integrity, gentleness, and strength." Maybe you feel happiest when you are being "sneaky glitter fun." Pick whatever mix of words feels right for you and gives you that feeling of "ah, that's me, and I like that."

_____

_____

_____

_____

_____

_____

_____

_____

_____

_____

_____

_____

MIDWAY CHECK-IN

Thinking about trauma and the way life can be unpredictable is challenging. How do you feel about it all in this moment? Do you feel curious and energized? Perhaps you feel overwhelmed and annoyed. Maybe it's something in between. Whatever it is, check in with yourself. Close your eyes or gaze softly at the floor if you'd like, and take a deep breath in, imagining it's coming from the bottom of your spine to the top of your head. This visualization helps focus your mind a little more than a normal inhale and exhale, and it helps ease anxiety. Hold that breath and relax your stomach, neck, and shoulders. When you decide it's time to let it out, let it out like you're blowing out a candle, long and slow. Keeping your eyes closed or your gaze soft, take your next breath in like you normally would. Stay in this space and check in with yourself again. How are you feeling? What do you need right now? What is a good idea for your next task today?

You might decide you'd like to read more or do one of the exercises. Or you might decide it's time to be done for now, for today, or even for the week. That's perfectly fine. What's important is that you listen to what is true for you.

Surviving Setbacks

Setbacks generally happen when you experience a challenge you hadn't planned or prepared for. Some setbacks are internal because there's a tool or skill you are either missing or need more practice with. External setbacks occur when other people or outside events interrupt your goals and growth. Internal setbacks tend to come up when your progress has been going well, but you suddenly find yourself feeling the same old way you used to. You might engage in behaviors you thought you had grown past. You might worry about concerns you have already worked through before. Potential setbacks are common early in healing, but they can also happen long after you have been living a new life for yourself. What's up with this?

The answer is: for the same reason healing isn't linear. Setbacks happen because you are a unique, complex, dynamic creature who encounters new things daily. Sometimes you have built yourself up well for what you know, but a new scenario you hadn't planned for or predicted pops up and challenges you all over again. Sometimes it's because you gain better perspectives to understand things that happened in your past as you learn and grow. Maybe you suddenly understand part of your traumatic experience that was previously confusing, and now you must process and cope with new details that have come to mind. These realizations can come with a flood of new emotions, even if you thought you had processed and moved on already.

Although this process is uncomfortable and may be annoying, it is an opportunity to continue your growth and strength in integrating and adapting to your experiences. When you find yourself in an internal setback like this, consider where you are in the three stages of healing. Would it serve you best to work again on your current safety and stability? You may find your everyday care routine has become inconsistent and chaotic. Or you may need to find ways to process, mourn, and express your feelings again. Maybe you are past both safety and mourning and just want to figure out what you want to do with your new understanding. It might just be an opportunity to work on skills and habits you'd rather have instead of the ones you've found yourself doing again. Whatever serves you best today is a great direction to explore.

You may also find that you encounter an external setback. You may have done everything you were supposed to, but you can't carry out the plan as intended because something disruptive happens in the world around you. It can be something small, like someone you were counting on can't help you with a project one day. It could be something large, like a natural disaster. Whatever it is, you find yourself with a plan that can't unfold the way you wanted it to. The timing of stressful events is unpredictable. It's easy to feel frustrated and disoriented when you have done everything you were supposed to, but things don't pan out the way you thought they would.

Unpredictability in the world is part of life. Your goals and plans are important, but they seldom (if ever) end up exactly how you had imagined. Many people feel like life is about finishing all their plans exactly as they'd intended. Life, instead, is more about what you do and how you grow when things don't go according to plan. The more you can be flexible, accept the things you cannot change, and move forward with your values in mind, the happier you'll be. You will find success in more places than you had first imagined.

When a setback happens, you may need to reevaluate your goals. Goals and the planned steps to them are a great basic outline for how you think you might succeed. Some goals are easy to follow through with because they are small, specific, and require a short period of time to reach. Even these goals may face unexpected setbacks. While you're working on an assignment, maybe your pen runs out of ink. If your goal is a longer-term goal, perhaps like earning a college degree, there is greater opportunity for interruptions, obstacles, and setbacks. You can't plan for every factor that will affect your goals. This is not failure; this is life. Each surprise, obstacle, or delay is an opportunity to pause and reassess what you are doing and if it will still serve you. You might find your goals still fit you perfectly. Or you may find they are no longer relevant to the life you want to live. You may even realize that you have unexpectedly made the life you wanted already! The more open you are to adapt to changes, accepting who you are, and growing continuously, the more likely you will find overall satisfaction. When you encounter a setback, take a moment to breathe and figure out your options. What comes next?

> "Life is more about what you do and how you grow when things don't go according to plan."

EXERCISE

This exercise will help you reflect on how you have adapted to new information and goal changes over time. Take a moment to remember when you were very young. What was the first job you wanted to do as an adult? What were the reasons you felt that way? Do you still have that same goal? If so, are your reasons the same, or have they developed deeper over the years? Have you become more specific in your interest? If you do not have the same goal, what changed your decision over time?

_____

_____

_____

_____

_____

_____

_____

_____

_____

_____

_____

_____

_____

MIDWAY CHECK-IN

It's time for a check-in. The world can be unpredictable, and you've learned how to manage setbacks you may encounter. People grow and change over time, and, as you do, it's important to reconsider your goals. How do you feel about this information? Have you seen this kind of challenge within your own life? What are some ways you may need to be flexible and adaptable in the future? How are you doing with creating safety and stability, mourning and managing your challenges, and building the life you want for yourself? The work you're doing is challenging and yet amazing. You are building new, stronger neuronal connections in your brain with every decision you make. Your brain learns from everything you do.

Take this opportunity to move around a bit, get a stretch, and do something grounding after all this thinking. What is something that immediately catches your attention as you look around? What is something around you that you forgot was there until just this moment? Do you smell or hear anything? What time of day is it? Most important, how do you feel right now? Would a snack or a glass of water be a good next choice? Perhaps it's time to take a break and talk to a friend about something fun. Honor and respect what serves you in this moment.

[Raj's Story]

Raj was determined not to let his traumatic experience compromise his future. He took his healing seriously and made plans for the life he wanted. He imagined himself graduating top of his class. He wanted to talk about his recovery from PTSD as an encouraging graduation speech. After all, if he had overcome his pain and challenges, surely others could succeed as well. He would go to his top choice of colleges and work helping others as an adult.

Because of an injury he had sustained during his trauma; however, Raj found himself needing more time to process information. This meant classwork required more effort, and he made unexpected mistakes. Understanding new concepts was tiring enough to frustrate Raj. It was difficult not to compare himself, not just to others, but to the old version of himself. How could he reach his goal of inspiring and helping others if he was struggling and stressed? The more pressure Raj felt, the harder it became to think clearly.

Raj had to admit his difficulties when explaining an incomplete assignment to a teacher. He felt ashamed, but his teacher took a more realistic approach. Raj's teacher reminded him of his injury and how strongly it must have affected his ability to think and process information. She reminded him that his challenges were not something to be ashamed of and that nobody would think less of him simply because life had gotten a little harder. It was a difficult concept for Raj to accept, but he knew in his heart it was true.

How to Reevaluate or Redefine Boundaries

Like goals, boundaries should serve your needs realistically and in the present. Boundaries are not one-size-fits-all forever. You may decide, for example, not to engage with social media at all early in your healing. You might need that space to be out of the social gaze and stay focused on your own needs instead of feeling pressured to pretend to be well. Over time, however, you might find you have gotten quite strong at handling your needs and are not as bothered by social media posts. You might decide to allow for a few minutes of social media engagement a day while being mindful about how it makes you feel.

There might be some people you are comfortable with within your social circle and even your support system. Over time, though, you may find they no longer feel fun or supportive, and they may challenge your ability to continue happy and healthy habits. It's appropriate and import-ant to recognize these changes and adjust your boundaries accordingly. You are both allowed to and responsible for deciding how you'd like to interact with others. Using the garden analogy on page 95, there are times when you need to close access to most people while you work on replant-ing and caring for your garden. If you don't allow yourself this downtime, you might become overwhelmed and burnt out from constantly engaging with others while your own needs go unnurtured. You are a living, breath-ing organism, and your needs will change over time. Boundaries exist to protect needs, so take time to adjust them as needed.

Check in with yourself regularly and listen to your needs. This will help you see when they shift and when your boundaries might need to be adjusted. You may find you are missing out on opportunities to grow because an old boundary keeps you away. Consider slow and gentle ways to open up to new and different experiences. If you avoided all parties with the goal of creating a calmer life but you now want to socialize more,

> ❝Boundaries exist to protect needs, so take time to adjust them as needed.❞

consider whether going to a smaller event for just twenty minutes is a good first step. Once you try it out, continue to adjust your decisions as needed. How did you feel in that setting? Do you feel like you were safe? If the experience was positive but you still feel nervous, that could be a sign that a gentle, slow approach is still a good idea.

What should you do if you find someone has crossed or challenged your boundaries? You might feel uneasiness or discomfort in your stomach or chest. Even if you don't understand why you feel bothered, this is a strong sign a boundary was crossed. Whether it's in the moment or later, as you think about it, take a deep breath and sigh it out. Now that your emotions have let you know the situation is not ideal, you'll want to think about this clearly.

First, think about your connection to this person. What's the purpose of engaging with them? Who have they been to you in the past? Is this a relationship you want to put work into? Communicating boundaries or healing a relationship after a boundary violation takes work. It's up to you to decide whether this work is appropriate or worth it to you. Second, think about the situation and what happened. If the interaction had gone better, what would have changed? Why did it bother you? For example, if someone calls you a hurtful name, the impact might depend on how close you felt to the person before that, and whether that comment touches an area you feel vulnerable about. Maybe if a stranger had said it, you would have laughed it off. That doesn't mean you don't have a right to be upset in this context. What would you have expected from this person?

Third, consider whether you have already expressed your boundaries to this person. If not, it may be worth voicing your needs in an honest but kind way. This gives them the opportunity to improve in the future. Voicing a boundary starts by taking ownership of your own feelings. This might sound like, "I've struggled with my grades in the past, so I'd appreciate it if you didn't make jokes about me failing. You might not have realized this before, but if it comes up again, I'll end the conversation." Assume best intentions when choosing your words. They might not have any idea they did something that bothered you. Or they might have difficulty remembering but are clearly working hard to do better.

Regardless of their intention, however, the fourth step is to follow through with what you said you would do next if it happens again. Ending a conversation or physically leaving a place is not a punishment for them but a measure of safety for you. It gives you room to process what happened and regroup. It allows you to make decisions that protect your needs. And in the end, the person who needs to respect your boundaries the most is you. You're worth it.

EXERCISE

An effective way of communicating needs and boundaries is using "I" language. "I" language presents concerns while acknowledging you are speaking from your own perspective. This might look like: "I felt hurt when you forgot my birthday because, to me, it meant I wasn't important to you." This is a great way to communicate your concerns without blaming others. It gives both people an opportunity to think about their relationship as well as how their perspectives may differ. Give it a shot by filling in the blanks:

"I felt _____

when you _____

because, to me, it meant _____

_____."

"I felt _____

when you _____

because, to me, it meant _____

_____."

"I felt _____

when you _____

because, to me, it meant _____

_____."

EXERCISE

Thinking creatively helps with processing and self-expression. Going back to the "garden of your life" analogy on page 95, consider how that landscape has changed over time. You are given this garden when you are born, and it changes as you grow and experience life. It already has different kinds of plants and animals that live in it. What sorts of plants? What colors? Flowers, vegetables, or trees? Cacti? Birds? Fish? Get as creative as you want in describing your garden. How would you describe what happened to your garden during your traumatic experience? After the event, what has changed? Are some changes permanent or temporary? Regardless of the event, how would you like to change your garden moving forward?

_____

_____

_____

_____

_____

_____

_____

_____

_____

_____

MIDWAY CHECK-IN

It can be stressful to reassess your needs and your connections to others. Letting go of people who have been important to you is hard! Remembering how you have been hurt or had your needs ignored can be painful all over again. But the short-term discomfort of these tasks will guide you in honoring your long-term needs. Be proud of yourself—the work you've done in this chapter is challenging but vital. The more you hear and respect the pain you have, the sooner it will heal. Being a human is complicated enough; being a human in relationship to others adds a whole new layer. That's why maintaining healthy connections and letting go of those that no longer serve you are both important to your long-term well-being.

Give yourself a nice stretch and a deep breath. If you have privacy, let yourself make whatever yelling or groaning or muttering sounds you feel inside as you exhale. You could also do this into a pillow to muffle the sound. Letting yourself release those sounds can feel relieving and cathartic. Now take another breath in through your nose and then immediately out through your nose. You have handled so many things. You are so capable. Tune in to what your body needs in this moment, like some movement or nap or snack, and honor that need.

[*Jace's Story*]

Jace felt like his world stopped at the point of his traumatic experience. He felt increasingly disconnected, as his symptoms kept him stuck in trauma. Jace had felt overwhelming anger about his experience and constantly wished that it could be erased. What about all his plans? What about his expectations for how the world was supposed to work? Why couldn't everything just go back to how it was? As he began to work through treatment for PTSD, however, his "stuckness" slowly loosened and gave him room to exhale, a little at a time. He learned to recognize his needs and express his feelings. He learned how to advocate for the person he wanted to become. As he reflected on himself and his experience a year and a half later, he came to realize how much he had healed and grown as a person. The journey of processing his experience and determining his personal values had kept him busy and focused. Jace reconnected with his life, his peers, and his family. The traumatic event and the person Jace was immediately after felt like a whole lifetime away from where he was now.

And while he would never choose to repeat his traumatic experience, Jace realized he no longer felt the need for it just to disappear. It had happened, and Jace had found a way to move forward. Not every day was easy, but Jace realized that navigating hardship and finding peace again was a common piece of life he could definitely manage.

How You Can Help End the Trauma Cycle

Even if you feel isolated, you are not alone in your trauma. Other people have experienced similar struggles and can understand your challenges. Unfortunately, people who have been hurt may, in turn, hurt others. This is because of how unresolved trauma affects us and how we interact with others.

Trauma affects and changes the way we view ourselves, other people, and the world around us. It fractures healthy connections and replaces peace with pain and disorientation. If you don't receive appropriate support and healing but instead accept the painful messages trauma has left you with as truth, you'll respond to yourself, others, and the world around you accordingly. A traumatic experience may give you the idea that you are helpless. If you don't later learn to recognize your own strength, you may never take the initiative and instead lose many opportunities to live a fulfilling life. You may take your anger out on others, hoping it will help you feel better. Harsh messages come from harsh experiences. Unchecked, these negative lessons create a vision of the world that seemingly justifies harsh behavior.

Although trauma may teach negative lessons, it rarely provides us with appropriate skills to achieve our goals. A child who is mistreated by their parents, for example, may grow up without knowledge of how to appropriately raise a child. As an adult, that person may also still struggle with the kinds of emotional management and personal values development they could have learned from healthy parents. Therefore, that person is more likely to struggle to teach their own children adaptive life skills. Their child might then grow up vulnerable to the same struggles. They may not know effective ways to manage their emotions and may, instead, take them out on others in an attempt to feel better.

And the cycle continues until someone recognizes the pain and difficulty they have gone through and decides to learn and grow to do better. Until someone is willing and able to be honest and vulnerable. Until someone accepts that life can be different and wants to work toward something better.

It can be a large decision, like separating from a toxic family and building a life of peace and healing. It can be a small decision, like choosing to be kind and gentle to yourself and others even though someone cut in front of you in line. It's knowing that "everyone else" around you may be choosing careless or harmful behaviors, but you are choosing to be different. The cycle continues until someone like you ends it.

The world can be overwhelming. Natural disasters, wars, injustice, poverty, and cruelty challenge and cause difficulty for many people. And, yet, among all the turmoil and darkness and pain, there has always been life. There have always been people who have struggled in some way but continued to build the life that best served them, their communities, and their children. There have been amazing human advancements in science, technology, and art. Humans have found ways to laugh and cry together, persevere through challenges, and create pockets of light and joy and kindness in the middle of it all.

This is a miracle of humanity. There is always the chance for healing and amazing cycle-breakers to come and change things. People who say, "I know what happened to me, and I won't let that happen to others. At the very least, not because of me." When you choose to heal your wounds, you change the patterns of life around you. If someone says something rude to you, it's easy for it to affect your mood negatively. You then might end up acting grumpy around others, which might make their own grumpiness flare up. Next thing you know, everyone is grumpy. Or maybe instead, you hear that rude comment, and you choose to say something nice to the next person you see. Something you would've liked to have heard yourself. That person's day becomes a little brighter, and they are more likely to share that energy with others as well. The small things matter!

Even setting boundaries affects others in positive ways. Sure, some people may feel angry if your boundary disrupts their expectations of how they could treat you. However, this can be an eye-opener and may encourage them to learn better skills, either now or in the future. Some may feel inspired by the positive changes and healing you're making in your life. You don't even need to tell people what you are changing—they may simply notice the difference in you. Perhaps they notice your peace, your happiness, and the way you handle yourself in difficult times. They then might try the same healthier behavior for themselves. It's like lighting a match in a dark room: The room may still be mostly dark, but the light is undeniable.

> **"When you choose to heal your wounds, you change the patterns of life around you."**

EXERCISE

Get your brain flowing with new possibilities. Take five minutes to quickly write, type, or record as many activities you could do next year as possible. Don't stop to think about it too much. Pick things that are both realistic and unrealistic. The goal is to let the ideas flow and get as many as possible. "Eat a sandwich as big as my face." "Fly a plane." "Go camping." "See bears." "Be invited into a bear family." "Paint bears." Now look at your list. You could do any of these things. You could choose none of them. The world is open to you.

- _____

- _____

- _____

- _____

- _____

- _____

- _____

- _____

- _____

- _____

CLOSING CHECK-IN

It's understandable if one of the last things you want to do is talk about and remember awful things, but I hope you have found freedom and relief in working through this book. I hope you have felt understood and not alone and that perhaps you are feeling a sense of peace and freedom right now as you consider the possibilities of life. Just like unexpected negative events can occur, so can unexpected positive events. Not knowing what the future holds can be challenging and even scary, because it could be anything. At the same time, it can be exciting and full of promise, because it could be anything! The reasons you might feel nervous can be the same reasons you are excited. The obstacles that get in the way of your goals can become the checklist of steps to handle to reach those same goals. Because you're the narrator of your own story, you get to decide how you view yourself, the world, and your experience. You also get to explore what comes next.

You might have reached this final check-in by reading the whole book, or because you are reading sections that seem interesting to you, or even because you've just opened and skimmed these pages for the first time. Regardless of how these words find you, you are an amazing person who has been through challenges and trials in life. It doesn't matter whether you wake up every morning ready to take on the world, or you wake up and realize this is a stay-in-bed kind of day. Your persistence in every moment of life is beautiful and worth respecting. Life is weird and tough, and none of us signed up for this on purpose: We just showed up one day with no idea what to expect. But there's a lot of good out there, and you get to choose what your life means to you. Your learning and growth up to this point are phenomenal. That doesn't mean you have to pull off some huge, life-changing goal every day. Living in your moment and being who you are is enough.

Take a nice stretch and pay extra attention to where you are stiff or sore. If you're able to, spend some extra moments shaking out or moving your limbs however they would like to be moved. Take in a big, deep breath, and let it out any way you want to. Breathe and spend some time just being in your space, in your body, and tune in to what you need right now. A snack? A drink of water? Another stretch? A fun conversation with someone you care about? Quality time with a pet? Honor your needs.

Key Takeaways

You've reached the end of chapter 5—well done! In this last chapter of the book, you looked at what you might expect for the future. You explored ways to troubleshoot challenges you might face and adjustments you may need to make. Hopefully, you feel more prepared to explore life and continue to build your own experiences, perspectives, and strengths. The future is unpredictable. But you have tools. And you are strong. Your confidence in your ability to continue forward and overcome obstacles will serve you well.

- Healing isn't a one-and-done kind of situation. It looks different from person to person. People experience trauma, healing, and life in general in unique ways. Because of this, try not to compare where you are to others. Instead, just tend to your present experience and needs as they arise. You might find yourself having different needs from day to day or needing to revisit skills you've used in the past. This is normal and to be expected. You'll get better at it with practice.

- Setbacks are part of the healing process. It's impossible to guess every potential outcome and event you will experience. Feelings and experiences you had previously resolved may come back up for you, along with negative feelings. When this happens, this is an opportunity to practice healthy skills again and become even stronger.

- External setbacks can also throw you off your game. Sometimes you face obstacles despite your best work and effort. It's nobody's fault that you can't predict and plan for every possible event—there are infinite possibilities in every moment. Adaptability requires acceptance and flexibility in your goals. Is there a new way you can accomplish what you want? Will you still complete your goal, just in a different time frame? Is your goal still relevant to you? You're allowed to change your mind and your plans.

- Much like goals, boundaries also deserve review and adjustment from time to time. Boundaries serve to protect your needs, and needs fluctuate. As you heal and grow throughout life, you will go through periods of time where you need to be more protective of your health and well-being. Other times, you may find your previous boundaries have become overly restrictive. Keep tuned in to what you need, and practice voicing your boundaries to others. Regardless of their response, your needs and boundaries are yours to protect.

- People with unresolved trauma may harm and traumatize others, intentionally or unintentionally. The result is a cycle in which people who are hurting and don't have the adaptive skills to heal and improve continue to hurt others. When you empower yourself to heal from your trauma, you break that cycle of harm and create more good in the world. Your interactions with others become healthier, which in turn inspires improvement in your own interactions. There's a lot of trauma in the world, but you can help create cycles of healing, healthy connection, and peace.

You've reached the conclusion of this workbook. Congratulations! I hope you feel encouraged and better equipped to move forward from your traumatic experience and build a life you enjoy. There will be tough times, wonderful times, and boring times. You will build new connections and say goodbye to others. Although I can't tell you how everything in life will happen, I can say it will be so much easier if you stay open to learning and growing. Be kind and gentle to yourself. Enjoy the small things in the moments you have. Breathe through the discomfort of hard times and know they are temporary. Remember your strength, your abilities, and your joy. This book will be here for you to revisit whenever you need it. This conclusion, like every conclusion, is also a new beginning.

Resources

The following resources can help you learn more about PTSD and healing.

National Child Traumatic Stress Network
nctsn.org/audiences/youth
Provides many videos and guides to help teens understand and cope with trauma.

Coalition for Immigrant Mental Health
ourcimh.org/mh-resources
Online resources for immigrant and refugee youth are usually regional or geared toward educating regional organizations. Although it is currently limited, CIMH's list may be a good starting point for finding resources including crisis counseling hotlines.

Crisis Connections
crisisconnections.org
Confidential and anonymous help lines for when you need to talk to someone; check their website for current numbers.

The National Suicide Prevention Lifeline (United States)
1-800-273-TALK (8255)
24/7 hotline providing free, confidential support for anyone in distress.

Stop It Now!
stopitnow.org/ohc-content/crisis-hotlines-for-youth
Dedicated to stopping child and teen abuse; specialized hotlines for different topics and concerns.

The Trevor Project
thetrevorproject.org
Community, informational resources, and crisis support for LGBTQ
young people.

Some Helpful Books

*Hello Cruel World: 101 Alternatives to Suicide for Teens, Freaks, and Other Out-
laws* by Kate Bornstein
A beautifully vulnerable and unorthodox book for the dark and difficult
moments in life. If you're a bit unconventional and experience suicidal
ideation, you might appreciate this book.

*The DBT Skills Workbook for Teens: A Fun Guide to Manage Anxiety and Stress,
Understand Your Emotions, and Learn Effective Communication Skills*
by Kristen Dahlin
DBT is not directly related to trauma and PTSD, but it teaches many great
skills for teens to learn and practice. You'll learn about and practice mind-
fulness and making wise decisions, distress tolerance, emotion regulation,
and interpersonal effectiveness.

The Comfort Book by Matt Haig
Matt Haig has a wonderful way of writing comforting and optimistic books.
This book is a collection of his thoughts, stories, and observations over
time that may bring reassurance and a gentle sense of hope.

*Trauma Treatment Toolbox for Teens: 144 Trauma-Informed Worksheets and
Exercises to Promote Resilience, Growth & Healing* by Kristina Hallett and
Jill Donelan
An in-depth collection of tools to practice toward understanding your
experience and healing your PTSD.

*PTSD Survival Guide for Teens: Strategies to Overcome Trauma, Build Resilience,
and Take Back Your Life* by Sheela Raja
Discussion about PTSD and example stories, along with tips for managing
symptoms and building resilience.

Looking over many of the resources listed above for teens may help you in your own understanding and support of their healing. *The DBT Skills Workbook* provides information and skills you can practice together. Use of these skills may also help you in your own emotional management and communication during this challenging time. Reading and discussing Matt Haig's uplifting book together may help you share in mutual optimism and support for a hopeful life to come.

Additional Resources for Caregivers

The Center for Child Trauma Assessment, Services, and Interventions through Northwestern University's Fenberg School of Medicine
cctasi.northwestern.edu/parents-caregivers
Answers questions you may have about supporting your teen through the trauma they've experienced.

The Child Welfare Information Gateway
childwelfare.gov/topics/responding/trauma/caregivers
Provides resources to help you support teens and children who have experienced traumatic events.

The National Child Traumatic Stress Network
nctsn.org/audiences/families-and-caregivers
Provides guides to support you in understanding and helping teens recover.

References

Abdul-Hamid, Walid Khalid, and Jamie Hacker Hughes. "Nothing New under the Sun: Post-Traumatic Stress Disorders in the Ancient World." *Early Science and Medicine* 19, no. 6 (2014): 549–557.

Brown, C. Brené. *The Gifts of Imperfection: Let Go of Who You Think You're Supposed to Be and Embrace Who You Are.* Center City, MN: Hazelden Publishing, 2010.

Chomsky, Noam. *Knowledge of Language: Its Nature, Origin, and Use.* New York, NY: Praeger, 1986.

Herman, Judith Lewis. *Trauma and Recovery: The Aftermath of Violence, from Domestic Abuse to Political Terror.* New York, NY: Basic Books, 2015.

Kaya, Aylin, Derek K. Iwamoto, Jennifer Brady, Lauren Clinton, and Margaux Grivel. "The Role of Masculine Norms and Gender Role Conflict on Prospective Well-Being among Men." *Psychology of Men & Masculinities* 20, no. 1 (2019): 142.

Levine, Peter A. *Waking the Tiger: Healing Trauma.* Berkeley, CA: North Atlantic Books, 1997.

Siegel, Daniel J. *Developing Mind, Third Edition: How Relationships and the Brain Interact to Shape Who We Are.* Guilford Publications, 2020.

———. "What Is the Mind?" Posted 2012. TEDxSunsetPark video, 19:10. youtube.com/watch?v=Ak5GCyBFY4E.

Siegel, Daniel J., and Tina Payne Bryson. *The Whole-Brain Child: 12 Revolutionary Strategies to Nurture Your Child's Developing Mind.* New York: Bantam, 2012.

Young, Yvette, Kim Korinek, Zachary Zimmer, and Tran Khanh Toan. "Assessing Exposure to War-Related Traumatic Events in Older Vietnamese War Survivors." *Conflict and Health* 15, no. 1 (2021): 1–16.

"Understanding the Teen Brain." Health Encyclopedia. University of Rochester Medical Center, n.d. urmc.rochester.edu/encyclopedia /content.aspx?ContentTypeID=1&ContentID=3051.

Index

About the Author

Dr. Stephanie Bloodworth, PsyD (she/her/hers), is a licensed marriage and family therapist. She has researched covert masculine supremacy and its relationship with women's models of strength. She works in solo private practice in Houston and specializes in supporting people who are tired of always being the "strong" one for everyone else. She presents at various local professional organizations, speaking about her specialties as well as her experience as an AAPI mental health professional. She has lived in Taiwan, California, and Missouri and currently lives in Texas with her husband. They might move to Canada. Outside of the therapy room, Stephanie enjoys technology, reading, practicing making art, and trying not to work too much.

CPSIA information can be obtained
at www.ICGtesting.com
Printed in the USA
BVHW012110270623
666477BV00001B/4